Improving Convention Center Management Using Business Analytics and Key Performance Indicators

Improving Convention Center Management Using Business Analytics and Key Performance Indicators

Advanced Practices

Myles T. McGrane

BEP

BUSINESS EXPERT PRESS

Leader in applied, concise business books

Improving Convention Center Management Using Business Analytics and Key Performance Indicators: Advanced Practices

First published in 2020 by
Business Expert Press, LLC
222 East 46th Street, New York, NY 10017
www.businessexpertpress.com

ISBN-13: 978-1-95253-806-3 (paperback)
ISBN-13: 978-1-95253-807-0 (e-book)

Business Expert Press Tourism and Hospitality Management Collection

Collection ISSN: 2375-9623 (print)
Collection ISSN: 2375-9631 (electronic)

First edition: 2020

10 9 8 7 6 5 4 3 2 1

Printed in the United States of America.

Abstract

I wrote this book because I believe convention centers can perform better. Many in senior management positions feel likewise and have a good sense of their center's potential for growth. As busy as they are, there's little time and resources available for thoughtful development of a fulsome management strategy to lift their center's performance. In our work environment it's common for management's attention to be diverted and overwhelmed by the small problems of the day. Meeting agendas where the latest event profit/loss statements are reviewed or sales leads discussed are often deferred. Why is this so? The principal cause is that operational and customer service data are not collected and organized in a form that is easy to follow, draw conclusions from and acted on. Action is most likely not data – based but rather based on intuition and gut feeling. How can management get past this, where can you turn?

The answer is to adopt and embrace business analytics and key performance indicators (KPIs). Improving Convention Center Management Using Business Analytics and Key Performance Indicators (both volumes) will guide you through that process. It introduces and rolls out sound practical advice from an author who has experienced and succeeded in what was one of the toughest work environments in our industry. Other KPI advice and "how to" books do not touch on the business and performance metrics unique to our industry. KPIs presently used are very general and only presented in publications such as annual reports.

I believe this book is best suited for the practitioners who work at convention centers or with a company that services convention centers. These are the individuals who make things work; managers at all levels, from senior leadership to floor supervisors. This book is also a useful resource for those in graduate schools of business or hospitality and hotel administration. It ties theory to actual practice. Others may find it interesting and informative too; political staff, city managers, hotel operators, bond underwriters and investors, engaged citizen groups, and all those businesses that either supply, service, or depend on convention center events.

Keywords

Convention Center (or Centre); Convention and Visitor Bureau (CVB); Convention and Exhibition Center; vertical market; Key Performance Indicator (KPI); tradeshow; occupancy rate; consumer show; net square footage; economic impact; hotel or hotel occupancy tax; economic feasibility study; exclusive contractor; earned revenue; social media presence; soft target; Wifi; license agreement; deferred maintenance; labor union grievances; event organizer; electric demand charges; Net Promoter Score (NPS); Workman's Compensation Fraud; Experience Modification Rating (EMR); Hotel room nights; Javits Center; IMPLAN

Contents

Introduction

Volume 1 focused on fundamental indicators that are essential to using business analytics and KPIs as a management strategy. Volume 2 expands the program introducing KPIs that I regard as important but more appropriate after fundamental KPIs have been tried. The KPIs in this volume are closely related to KPIs described in Volume 1. These "derivatives" represent a deeper dive into factors affecting Volume 1 KPIs. Know that in some circumstances derivatives may become very important. They are useful and can surprise—from time to time in my experience derivatives yielded more valuable and actionable data than fundamental KPIs.

Most of the chapters in this volume (1–4 and 6–9)) are composed and formatted the same as Volume 1, covering major business functions such as Convention Center Business Fundamentals, Earned Revenue Activities, Security and Safety, and so on. For each KPI the narrative follows the format noted below:

- KPI
- Owner
- Data Sources and Collection
- Reporting Frequency
- Why This KPI Is Useful
- Objective
- Managing Unfavorable Conclusions and Inferences
- How to Calculate and/or Organize Data (Sample work sheets may also be presented)
- Presentation Notes and Formats (Sample tables and graphics for presentation will be included in several KPI narratives. The graphics and tables shown in ithe book are not prescriptive. Rather, they show a variety of examples of presentations; some are clear and underatandable, others not so much). Chapter 10 in this volume "Presenting and Displaying KPIs" offers the best advice and examples for tables and graphics.

- Also, a section entitled "Things to Watch For: Nuances, Misinterpretations, and Cautions" may follow referencing the KPI subject matter.

There will be four other chapters that don't fit the format above:

- Chapter 5 is titled "KPIs Applied: The Case of the Declining Profit Margin." This chapter is a case study providing perspective and insight into the discipline and value of a thoughtful KPI program.
- Chapter 10 is titled "Presenting and Displaying KPIs." This chapter gives practical advice on incorporating numerical information into a report or presentation. It outlines the role of tables, graphs, charts, and sometimes text as formats. It focuses on methods so that KPI presentations are easily understood.
- Chapter 11 is titled "Framework and Context and Steps for Implementing a KPI Program." This chapter discusses the need to classify and organize KPIs into a framework of strategic and/or operational elements. It also introduces a step process for implementing a KPI program at your convention center.
- Chapter 12, "Last Word," is a discussion about why this book has been written and what may be the probable outcomes if a convention center implements a comprehensive KPI program.

CHAPTER 1

Convention Center Business Fundamentals: Derivatives

Space Use (Occupancy Rate)

KPI: Net Square Footage (NSF) vs. GSF Rented for Exhibit Halls—NSF/GSF Ratio

Owner	Sales Department
Data Sources and Collection	The Sales Department will maintain a record of NSF/GSF ratio. If the "KPI: Operating Profit or Loss Statements for Each Event" is used and its work sheets completed, then through linking spreadsheets using MS Excel, this KPI can be automatically updated very soon after each event
Reporting Frequency	Semi-annually or more frequently if data are collected by linking spreadsheets per the above.

Why This KPI Is Useful

There should be concern when occupancy of exhibit halls is stable, but NSF has declined. In a case like this, space is not being rented or used efficiently. If it recurs with a retained event, it's a sign that something is wrong; the economic sector may be weak or a retained event organizer may have a business problem selling space for exhibit booths. When NSF/GSF Rented ratio is declining and widespread one will also see unfavorable changes vs. plan in financial KPIs.

Objective

A favorable ratio would be 35 percent or higher. The example below in "How to Calculate and/or Organize Data" is not a favorable NSF/GSF Ratio.

Managing Unfavorable Conclusions and Inferences

A consistent decline in a retained event's NSF/GSF Ratio could lead to difficult decisions. In my time at the Javits Center we routinely measured retained events' NSF/GSF ratio. A low NSF/GSF ratio was cause for a discussion with event organizers regarding NSF decline. If we saw an event consistently fall below a certain ratio, after a time we'd move the event to less desirable space and possibly offer those dates to another event that was growing or a new event with a reliable record of high NSF. These were not easy decisions. Event organizers took these decisions very hard. For most, the regular assignment of space adjacent to a grand lobby and attractive concourse was regarded as a major business asset. Organizers also regarded a shift in regular dates as a significant business problem.

How to Calculate and/or Organize Data

1. Sum NSF and GSF for each exhibit hall for the six-month period.
2. Per the example below, divide the Six-Month Total NSF /Six-Month Total Exhibit Hall GSF Rented = NSF/GSF Ratio
3. Say the NSF for the first six months of 2019 was 5,251,850 and the GSF for those rented exhibit halls was17,235,000. Then:
   - Exhibit Hall NSF (Jan.–June) is 5,251,850 sq. ft. /17,235,000 sq. ft.
   - NSF/GSF Ratio is 5,251,850/17,235,000=30.4%

Presentation Notes and Formats

Table, bar or line graph with table, comparing current year-to-date (YTD) to previous YTD. See the sample table (Table 1.1) and line graph (Figure 1.1) for a retained event NSF/GSF Ratio over seven years:

NSF/GSF RATIO - ROCKY MOUNTAIN CRAFTS FESTIVALS - SPRING AND FALL							
	2013	2014	2015	2016	2017	2018	2019
Rocky Mountain Crafts Festival - Spring	47.5%	48.0%	45.6%	39.2%	29.8%	26.5%	24.9%
Rocky Mountain Crafts Festival - Fall	51.8%	52.0%	49.4%	44.5%	37.3%	31.4%	27.3%

Table 1.1 NSF/GSF Ratio – Rocky Mountain Crafts Festivals – spring and fall

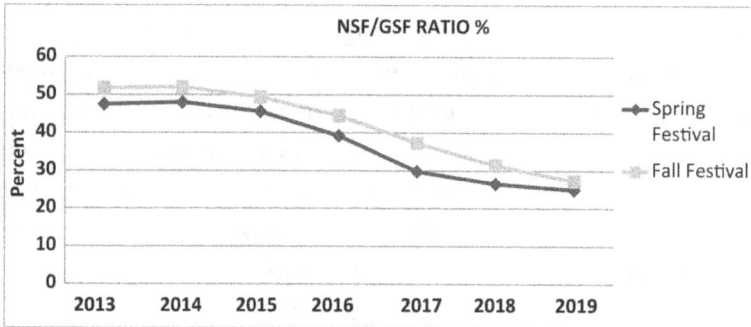

Figure 1.1 NSF/GSF Ratio – Rocky Mountain Crafts Festival – spring and fall

KPI—Occupancy Rate for Individual Spaces within Each Space Category

Owner	Sales Department
Data Sources and Collection	The Sales Department should establish and maintain an up-to-date record of occupancy rate by month for each rentable space
Reporting Frequency	Annually

Why This KPI Is Useful

Space is categorized as exhibit halls, meeting rooms, ballrooms, auditoriums, board rooms, and other. This KPI will show how well individual spaces within a category are occupied.

Objective

The objective is to find out when and which space category and individual space within the category are licensed the most frequently.

Managing Unfavorable Conclusions and Inferences

This KPI may confirm demand trends that are evident but some results may surprise. If demand is low and some spaces are simply very difficult to sell, then it's worthwhile finding out the event organizers' opinions. Opinions may include; the space configuration is wrong, the space is not contiguous with other exhibit halls, the look and feel of the space is not the same as other parts of the building, services such as restrooms, storage, and access to transportation are too far away and so on. At the Javits Center in the 1990s we had a similar situation with respect to meeting room suites that were poorly located and rarely rented. We solved this problem by hiring a talented design team to upgrade the carpets, finishes, and lighting, which worked surprisingly well.

When demand is high for long periods some may see this as an opportunity to explore variable pricing based on demand. Operating a convention center where the demand varies widely from season to season, but rental and service prices are relatively low and fixed is an inefficient sales model. When we graph demand vs. price, the inefficiency of fixed

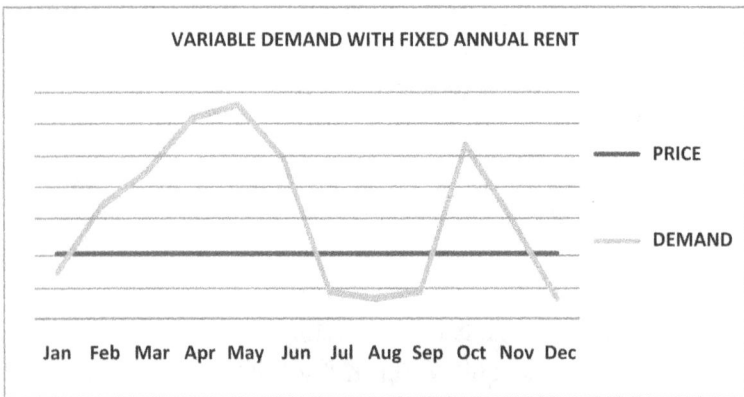

Figure 1.2 Variable demand with fixed annual rent

pricing is apparent. Figure 1.2 above is a figurative graph demonstrating the substantial seasonal variation of demand vs. fixed rent prices throughout the year.

For convention centers with occupancy rates above 60 percent, there are seasons when space rent is worth more to the market—yet rent and other fees remain the same throughout the year. Variable, dynamic, or demand pricing has become common and very profitable for hotels, major amusement parks, the airlines, Uber and Lyft, and many more businesses. Will this model work for convention centers? The analogy for those businesses to convention centers fits conceptually. However those businesses operate at high volume with thousands of customers every day. Importantly, most center managers will be wary that variable pricing will result in lost business. There are too many cities and venues that compete on the basis of price, i.e., low rent. Variable pricing may have a place but probably not in the same fashion as other business sectors. I recommend developing a pricing plan for times when high demand occurs consistently. Calculate the increased revenue possibilities. If it looks as if variable pricing will benefit your center with acceptable risk, transition into variable rent gradually and don't overreach.

How to Calculate and/or Organize Data

1. As an example, Occupancy Rate for Exhibit Hall A in 2019 = Annual GSF Rented for Hall A × # of days /Annual GSF available for Hall A × # of days.
2. Annual Occupancy Rate Exhibit Hall A = 50,000 GSF Rented × 194 days/ 50,000 GSF × 350 days =9,700,000/17, 500,000 = 55%
3. See Work Sheet 1.1:

OCCUPANCY RATE PER SPACE CATEGORY (%)			
	2017	2018	2019
Exhibit Halls			
Hall A	56	54	55
Hall B	50	48	49
Hall C	42	35	41
Meeting Rooms			
MR 100	57	56	51
MR 200	50	51	51
MR 300	46	46	46
MR 400	44	42	41
MR 500	35	37	37
Ballrooms			
Grand	13	36	17
Junior	20	20	22

Work Sheet 1.1 Occupancy rate per space category (%)

Presentation Notes and Formats

Table, bar graph, or both, comparing current and previous years.

Things to Watch for: Misinterpretations, Nuances, and Cautions

A Consistent History of Low NSF/GSF Ratios Overall Diminishes the Value of Using Occupancy Rate and GSF Rented as KPIs: Imagine a 100,000 gross square foot column-less exhibit hall .The maximum amount of net square footage achievable (given 10 ft. aisle widths) is between 55,000 and 65,000 NSF. An overhead photo of the hall with 62,000 NSF would easily confirm a filled space. Envision the amount of service revenue this situation yields. Now, imagine that same hall with 15,000 net square feet used. If overall service revenues are low, but fundamental KPIs like occupancy rate or number of events are high, the problem is usually low NSF.

Financial Reports

KPI: Amount and Percentage of Non-operating Revenue to Cover Losses

Owner	Finance Department
Data Sources and Collection	The Monthly Financial Report
Reporting Frequency	Monthly

Why This KPI Is Useful

Non-operating revenues are subsidies paid normally from hotel taxes and government tourism funds. They are paid to cover operating losses when earned revenue is less than expenses. An example of how this accounted for and recorded can be found in Volume 1 under Non-operating Revenues in Work Sheet 1a—Monthly Financial Report.

A growing percentage of loss coverage from subsidies is an unfavorable sign. This trend magnifies business risk if subsidy funds are limited, capped, or possibly diverted to other public projects.

Objective

Decrease the amount and percentage of non-operating revenue needed to cover operating losses.

Managing Unfavorable Conclusions and Inferences

A strong effort needs to be made to increase earned revenues. The effort has to be comprehensive, relying on KPIs which measure sales performance, service productivity, and pricing gaps when compared to competitors. Take steps to improve the performance of each category of KPIs. I would also take time to learn about the long-term reliance on subsidies. There are competing interests for hotel tax revenues elsewhere in some cities. Know that the advocacy and intensity of debate over this issue are growing.

How to Calculate and/or Organize Data

1. No calculation is necessary to obtain the amount.
2. To calculate percentage, sum annual earned revenue and the amount of non-operating revenue used to cover operating losses; then divide non-operating revenue used to cover operating losses by the sum. The quotient is the percent of non-operating revenue needed annually to cover operating losses.

Presentation Notes and Formats

Table, bar graph, or both, comparing current to previous years.

Economic Impact

KPI: Comparing Targeted Market Economic Impact to Other (Non - Targeted Market) Events

Owner	Sales Department
Data Sources and Collection	The Sales Dept. is the source of this information and data.
Reporting Frequency	Every 3 years

Why This KPI Is Useful

Enumerating and re-examining the value of targeted markets is essential for carrying on a long term sales and marketing strategy. Targeted markets are those that have an affinity for the city's economic base, can enhance the city's economic development plans, have a high probability of selecting your city and venue, and have an above average economic impact.

Objective

Develop a knowledge base for targeted markets (aka vertical markets). Use this KPI to measure and re-assess and compare the economic impact strength of targeted market events.

Managing Unfavorable Conclusions and Inferences

It would be an unfavorable revelation to learn that the targeted markets have a limited impact on the city and a below-average probability of selecting your city and venue. If this is the case, review the rationale behind the current target market selection with the CVB. If the rationale is deemed sound, ask why the probability for booking more targeted market events is so low? Is it something you can control and change or something else?

How to Calculate and/or Organize Data

1. Sum all targeted market events and non -targeted market events separately.
2. Sum economic impact (in $), the nimber of exhibitors and attendees from out-of-town and the amount of hotel room nights for targeted and non-targeted market events separately.
3. To obtain the averages per event for metrics in 2. above for targeted and non - targeted market events divide all by the nimber of events for targeted and non-targeted market events separately.

Presentation Notes and Formats

Table showing the summary of results. See Table 1.2 below

ECONOMIC IMPACT SUMMARY OF TARGETED MARKETS VS. NON-TARGETED MARKETS		
	Targeted Market Ave.	Non -Targeted Market Ave.
# of Events	50	115
Total Economic Impact	35,016,000	65,464,670
Ave. Econ. Impact/Event	700,320	569,258
NOTE: Alternatively one can choose to use or combine the "short version" of assessing economic imapct below		
# of Events	50	115
Out - of - Town Exhibitors and Attendees	18,700	28,800
Ave. Out-of-Town Exhibitors and Attendees/Event	374	250
Hotel Room Nights	28,100	43,150
Ave. Hotel Room Nights/Event	562	375

Table 1.2 Economic impact summary of targeted makets vs. non-targeted markets

KPI: Hotel Average Daily Room Rate (ADR) and Revenue per Available Room (RevPar) Trends vs. Convention Center Out-of- town Attendance Staying at Hotels

Owner	Sales Department
Data Sources and Collection	The city hotel association with assistance from the CVB
Reporting Frequency	Annually

Why This KPI Is Useful

ADR is a hotel's average daily room rate. RevPar is average room revenue per available room. RevPar is calculated by multiplying a hotel's ADR by its occupancy rate. It does not include food and beverage or other ancillary revenues generated by a hotel. Both ADR and RevPar are regarded as reliable KPIs in the hotel industry.

For convention centers, this KPI is not well established but for many of us it is a theory with merit. If convention center occupancy and the number of attendees staying at hotels materially contributes to hotel ADR and RevPar, then there is a solid statistic that can be incorporated into feasibility studies and add to the economic impact of convention center events. Academic researchers and consultants in the feasibility study business have not been particularly drawn to this theory. However, in 2010 HVS, a well-known consultancy, introduced the subject in a newsletter article "How Convention Centers Influence Hotel Markets." The article recognized the importance of convention center events and the impact or "price effect" they have on ADR and RevPar. HVS recommended using regression models to measure the impact of convention centers on their surrounding hotel markets. They developed an equation where the dependent variable of Number of Occupied Rooms is calculated by three independent variables (month of the year, weekday, and city-wide conventions). In 2018, an article in the online magazine *Hotel News Now* did provide actual statistics in a brief case study of the effect of Nashville's Music City Convention Center opening on ADR (43% increase) and RevPar (62% increase). It is acknowledged the statistics are few and sometimes inconsistent. However, given the characteristics of a hotel's time-based or dynamic pricing, both ADR and RevPar should track and trend similar to changes in convention center occupancy and out-of-town event attendees. This KPI may be best implemented when there is a new or expanded convention center event. If proven, convention centers can count on this trend as a clear demonstration of economic impact.

Objective

Statistically prove the correlation between high center occupancy and event attendance and higher hotel room prices. If proven, track, report and enumerate the results in dollars as an economic impact. If the correlation is low and inconsistent, discontinue this KPI.

Managing Unfavorable Conclusions and Inferences

As noted, if the outcome showing a low correlation between event attendees staying at hotels and ADR and RevPar is reason to drop this KPI. The relationship between two variables is generally considered strong when their "value correlation" is larger than 0.8.

How to Calculate and/or Organize Data

1. Organize statistics for the number of attendees staying overnight in hotels by calendar days for a one-month period. Do so in table form on an Excel spreadsheet.
2. Obtain ADR and RevPar statistics and organize in like fashion.
3. Calculate correlation using Excel Formula tab, click More Functions, click Statistics, click CORREL, and follow instructions.
4. If the correlation is strong, continue this procedure for another five months and review results. If the correlation is not strong, then discontinue this KPI. At some point the difference between ADR and RevPar when there are and are not events will have to be calculated and added to economic impact.
5. See Work Sheet 1.2:

EVENT ATTENDEE HOTEL STAYS CORRELATED TO HOTEL ADR AND REVPAR			
Month and Date	Attendees at Hotels	ADR	RevPar
Jan. 3	3,000	190	120
Jan. 4	3,500	190	120
Jan. 5	2,900	185	117
Jan. 8	1,500	176	115
Jan. 9	1,200	165	109
Jan. 12	5,400	210	123
Jan. 13	5,400	210	123
Jan. 14	5,500	214	125
Jan. 15	4,600	200	118
Jan. 16	900	187	110
Jan. 17	850	187	118
Jan. 20	4,380	209	129
Jan. 21	4,300	209	128
Jan. 22	3,544	200	127
Jan. 25	1,358	197	115
Jan. 26	1,233	183	113
Jan. 27	1,003	183	106
Jan. 30	945	175	102
Jan. 31	724	175	100
Correlation			
Attendees at Hotels to ADR		0.86	
Attendees at Hotels to RevPar		0.81	

Work Sheet 1.2 Event attendee hotel stays correlated to hotel ADR and RevPAR

Presentation Notes and Formats

Use tables during a six-month trial. If this KPI is to be continued, consider a graphic display of correlation results per month using a line or bar graph.

KPI: Jobs Created as a Result of Convention Center Events

Owner	Sales Department
Data Sources and Collection	Unless your staff or the CVB is familiar with the depth and measures (location quotients, employment multipliers, etc.) used by the Bureau of Economic Analysis I would rely on the consultant who performed the economic feasibility study for the center. The convention center's role is to validate or affirm event attendance.
Reporting Frequency	Annually

Why This KPI Is Useful

The contribution of convention center events to local employment is normally expressed as the number of jobs per $1 million in economic output. To give some perspective, the number of jobs created by the operation of the Las Vegas Convention Center (LVCC) is 6.3 jobs per $1 million in economic output for an area defined as Southern Nevada. In 2018 LVCC's economic output was $2.2 billion, and 13,860 jobs were created or supported if they already exist. If the economic model your consultants use is IMPLAN, then this includes full-time, part-time, and seasonal jobs. A recent article about the Washington State Convention Center (WSCC) expansion in Seattle claimed 11.5 new jobs per $1 million in economic output. This seems exaggerated as the WSCC is smaller than LVCC and the number if events is much less. For a smaller convention center like the Lancaster County Convention Center (LCCC) in Pennsylvania, the jobs created for both Lancaster city and county as a result of the center's business operations was 2.6 jobs per $1 million in economic output. In 2018, with an economic output of $196.7 million, 516 jobs were created.This gives you a range knowing that LVCC is probably near the top of the range, and LCCC is below the average. Familiarity with jobs created or supported by convention center events is an important metric for senior management. Jobs have a more down-to-earth connection to the public than indirect or induced spending or hotel room nights.

Objective

Use economic impact calculations to periodically report on the center's contribution to local employment. Express employment contributions as "jobs supported" and, if applicable "jobs created".

Managing Unfavorable Conclusions and Inferences

A decline in the number of jobs created or the expected rate of job growth means that economic output declined. If the number of events and the GSF Rented are doing well, I would first review the other fundamental KPIs and see if those indicators have in turn declined, especially the ones that deal with the event types and economic sectors. There can be a wide difference in business and economic impact performance given the nature of event types and economic sectors. Also, review lost business reports and market share of targeted markets. If your KPI program is well executed and comprehensive, you will find the causes. Lastly, I recommend a discussion with the consultants who did the economic feasibility study and obtain their reaction and response.

How to Calculate and/or Organize Data

Rely on the jobs per $1 million in economic output from your convention center's economic feasibility study. Sometimes the number of jobs is expressed in reports and marketing pieces as if the jobs were created during the time the report covers (like an annual report). You may consider expressing these jobs as "supported" rather than "created" unless there is a sharp increase in economic output that can be explained by event growth. This KPI should be updated every 3 to 5 years. This KPI is related to the Volume 1 "KPI: Economic Impact Due to Convention Center Events." The data can be displayed by adding rows for Jobs Created and Jobs Supported in Work Sheet 1.3 Annual Economic Impact (Chapter 1, Vol. 1) or reported separately.

Presentation Notes and Formats

Tables, bar graphs, or both, comparing current and previous years and business plan.

Things to Watch for: Misinterpretations, Nuances, and Cautions

The Owners of the IMPLAN Model Have a Caution about Designating "Created Jobs" Based on Indirect and Induced Spending from Convention Center Events: The paragraphs below (with sections italicized by the author by me) are from IMPLAN's Blog entitled: Employment FAQ," 2019:

> . . . we feel that, unless there are large numbers of jobs reported in the Indirect and Induced Effects, that *these impacts are largely supported rather than created.* This can be demonstrated by looking at the Detail Results of your impact and also by comparing the jobs associated to the impact to the current Employment in the impact sectors. Unless the change of Employment in the Indirect and Induced Effects are significant in comparison to the current Employment in the Sector, we recommend *considering it supported rather than created.* . . . many attempts have been made over the years to verify Indirect and Induced jobs, and this has proved very difficult to actually discern.[1]

This IMPLAN blog excerpt introduces another metric: "jobs supported." My view is that "jobs supported" is an implied indicator of job security for those in the city's hospitality sector and should be reported.

A Quiet KPI for a Convention Center's Economic Impact is Gaining Recognition: Progressive cities all have ambitious economic development plans. Typically plans focus on attracting innovative industries, establishing knowledge hubs (also called creative clusters), advancing the city's reputation for thought leadership in a particular field, and creating

---

[1] IMPLAN. 2019. "Employment FAQ." https://implanhelp.zendesk.com/hc/en-us/articles/115009510967-Employment-FAQ (accessed on December 2019).

a foundation for high-income employment. The presence of events in desirable sectors can support and favorably publicize this agenda. A convention center's economic impact should not be solely limited to direct spending and hotel room nights. There's something more. This idea was best expressed in a report from Skift (an online publication covering business travel and events). In their 2017 report "Defining Conventions as Urban Innovation and Economic Accelerators," they stated:

> Because science and technology are evolving at such a fast pace, cities have to expand their talent pools of professionals working in the STEM and creative industries more rapidly to remain competitive. Examples of those priority sectors include aerospace in Jacksonville, cleantech in Portland, bio-med in Denver, life sciences in San Diego, healthcare IT in Cleveland, cognitive media in Boston, and eSports in Washington, D.C. Conventions driving innovation in those demand sectors deliver companies and associations to a city's doorstep. Therefore, convention bureaus, governments, economic development consultants, academics, and researchers have face-to-face access with industry leaders to develop new business relationships, investments, research, and priority sector innovation.[2]

Be it real or an aspiration, certain event economic sectors booked by centers can be used to leverage a city's economic development plans. Applying this trend as a KPI for convention centers is not practical at this point, but anecdotal evidence of this trend is worth reporting in narrative form.

---

[2] Deventer, V., J. Paul, and H. Richard. 2017."Defining Conventions as Urban Innovation and Economic Accelerators." https://meetingsmeanbusiness.com/ sites/default/files/SkiftMMB-Defining-Conventions-As-Urban-Innovation-And-Economic-Accellerators-Report.pdf (accessed August 2019).

CHAPTER 2

Sales and Marketing Derivatives

KPI: Percentage of Contribution by Each Marketing Channel Resulting in Contract Execution

Owner	Sales Department
Data Sources and Collection	The Sales Department, the Social Media Manager, and the CVB will have all this information with annual results for all channel categories.
Reporting Frequency	Annually

Why This KPI Is Useful

This KPI records marketing channel contributions that result in a signed license agreement. Results from this data will inform marketing spending and investments and, most importantly, Sales Department's advertising expense and sales time allocated to each channel. While there are no industry benchmarks for comparison, there is plenty of published research on the channel contributions for digital marketing. The strongest digital marketing channels are consistently company websites and social media. For convention centers marketing effectiveness is measured by how well marketing strategies increase bookings. In our digital business world Marketing teams have access to real-time data, allowing for a very agile marketing strategy.

Objective

Find the most successful marketing channels, the ones that lead to signed license agreements.

Managing Unfavorable Conclusions and Inferences

Not applicable.

How to Calculate and/or Organize Data

1. Obtain and sum referrals for the following channel categories:
   - Hotelier referrals
   - Event organizer referral
   - Referral from others (General Service Contractors, consultant, and so on)
   - Response to an RFP
   - Facebook or LinkedIn page, Twitter feed, and so on.
   - E-mail campaigns
   - Promotional events (e.g., a cocktail party at an all industry event like Professional Convention Managers Association or Society of Independent Show Organizers)
   - Met or heard your sales staff speak at an event
   - Random general inquiry
   - Print ad (list publication)
   - Digital advertising (list specific placement source)
   - Industry rumor or news
   - Sales arranged meeting

To determine market channel percentage contribution follow this example:

2. Event Organizer Referrals/Total Executed Contracts = Percentage of Channel Contribution: 5 Referrals/180 Total Executed Contracts = 2.8%

Presentation Notes and Formats

See Table 2.1:

MARKETING CHANNEL CONTRIBUTION PERCENTAGE - RESULTING IN CLOSINGS		
Channel	%	Remarks
Hotelier Referrals	30	
Promotional events	21	PCMA dinner, SISO Cocktails
Event Organizer Referral	12	Reed, Nat'l Asso.of Reatilers
Referral from others	10	Freeman
Promotional events	10	Classic car auctions
Random Inquiry	7	Food festivals (2)
RFP Response	4	Informa, NAB
Social Media (Facebook, LinkedIn, etc.)	2	Our Facebook site and Blog
E-mail Campaign	1	Travel Show
Digital Ad	1	On TSNN website
Print Ad	1	Convene Mag
Industry rumor or news	1	Regarding Outdoor Retailers

Table 2.1 Marketing channel contribution percentage resulting in closings

KPI: Individual Performance Evaluations of the Sales Team

Owner	Human Resources Department and General Manager
Data Sources and Collection	The Head of Sales writes the performance reviews. The review for the Head of Sales is written by the General Manager
Reporting Frequency	Annually

Why This KPI Is Useful

This KPI is an in-depth analysis of individual performance, focusing on sales-manship and other personal qualities that contribute to sales. An example of personal qualities is how the individual comports themselves professionally with difficult and demanding clients. In many ways event organizers will form impressions of the city and convention center through its sales team.

It comes to this; it's the collective individual performance of the sales team that makes a successful, mediocre, or failing sales and marketing program. The measurements are the performance reviews must include specific business goals and objectives for those in sales.

Objective

Each sales team member performing above average.

Managing Unfavorable Conclusions and Inferences

Counseling, extra training, and if there is no improvement, some hard personnel decisions.

How to Calculate and/or Organize Data

No calculation is necessary.

Presentation Notes and Formats

Table showing overall performance and three other elements: client relations, qualified lead contributions, and contract closings (conversions). This KPI is confidential, meant only for senior level managers.

KPI: Summary of Website Performance

Owner	Social Media Manager or Communications Department
Data Sources and Collection	All data are supplied by the website host. Obtaining data about who is visiting your website and other information about them may be an extra expense.
Reporting Frequency	Quarterly

Why This KPI Is Useful

A convention center's website is integrated into so many aspects of business routine; it's hard to imagine operating without it. It is a fundamental marketing tool, a 24/7 communications site, an e-commerce site where orders and transactions are made, an information brochure to help people get around the city and a revenue generator if your center has an advertising and sponsorship program. If elected, your website can also be used to find out more about prospective event organizers and exhibitors: who they are, where they're from, and what they're interested in. You can track website performance by using a software tool like Google Analytics or use a more in-depth method provided by a Search Engine Optimization (SEO) company. A scope of service for an SEO company should include the following:

1. A security audit
2. A test of your website's compatibility with mobile devices
3. A test of the speed which your web pages load
4. The quality of your content
5. The ease of navigating from one page to another
6. The contribution or not of certain images, graphics, and excess text
7. The search intent of visitors
8. Identity and location of web users
9. As a minimum, measurement of these performance metrics:
   • Search engine ranking of overall traffic for your website vs. competitors
   • Search engine ranking of certain keyword searches for your website vs. competitors
   • Unique visitors
   • Returning visitors
   • Pages most visited
   • Geographic location of visitors (country and/or state)
   • Average time on site
   • Average page views
   • Convention center blog with opt-in email

Objective

Maintain a record of metrics that accurately reflect the event market, the freshness and appeal of the website, and its navigation and overall functionality. Another objective is for these metrics to compare favorably to B2B benchmark statistics.

Managing Unfavorable Conclusions and Inferences

Obtain an independent critique of your website.

How to Calculate and/or Organize Data

See sample Work Sheet 2.1:

WEBSITE PERFORMANCE			
	2017	2018	2019
Search Engine Traffic Ranking vs Competitors (%)			
Search Engine Keyword Ranking vs Competitors (%)			
Unique Visitors			
Returning Visitors			
Average Time on Site			
Average Page Views			
Blog opt-ins			
Pages Most Visited	CREATE TABLE LISTING OF TOP 5 or 10		
Location of Visitors (country or state)			

Work Sheet 2.1 Website performance

Presentation Notes and Formats

Tables, bar graphs, or both, comparing current YTD to previous YTD and B2B benchmark if found.

KPI: Social Media Presence

Owner	Communications Department and Social Media Manager
Data Sources and Collection	The Social Media Manager is responsible for composing some of the posts and is the point person for release and distribution. The manager always keeps count on the number of posts, followers of the posts, and likes and dislikes and replies.
Reporting Frequency	Quarterly

Why This KPI Is Useful

Developing a social media presence takes a thoughtful strategy and patience. This KPI tracks the readership and reaction and sentiment to content originated by the convention center. It enhances market visibility and may turn up opportunities that strengthen business reputation and growth if implemented properly. Presently a convention center's social media presence should include Facebook, LinkedIn, Instagram, YouTube, and Twitter. You should also publish a blog on a regular schedule and have opt-in email distribution and post the blog archive on your website. Your publication schedule should require frequent posts that are relevant and engage readers in a clear and interesting way. It's best to concentrate on original content and not a post of copied work from other sources unless it supports your original content. Also, avoid posting superficial puff pieces and do not overplay the sales message. The intent is to be responsive to questions and complaints and form a relationship with customers, from event organizers to exhibitors and other event participants such as contractors and stakeholders and all event attendees.

Objective

Create a social media presence that covers aspects of our business that are most on the minds of customers (existing and prospective), such as facility and service information, an up-to-date event calendar, new business initiatives, safety and security information, and so on. The sum of all this communication is to establish a brand that evinces professionalism, competency, innovation, and class leadership among convention centers and other major meeting venues. At some point it will be necessary to perform a competitive analysis. The objective is to become a leader in social media presence and measure its contribution in space sales and service sales, customer service, and business reputation.

Managing Unfavorable Conclusions and Inferences

There are several metrics that can gauge social media performance and you may find a relevant B2B benchmark or examples of other notable social media presence strategies. Work Sheet 2.2 will also be useful. At some point you will have accumulated enough data that will enable a reasonable self-evaluation. Your conclusion may well be that your social media presence needs improvement. B2B companies need to make judgments about the quantity and quality of those reading your posts. It may be that there are tangible results such as the acquisition of qualified leads. More often than not, the result is a self-evaluation, revamped social media strategy, or lessons learned.

How to Calculate and/or Organize Data

Keep track of social media presence by using a work sheet similar to the Work Sheet 2.2:

SOCIAL MEDIA PRESENCE - MARCH 2019							
Platform	Posts	Views	Downloads	Followers	Shares	Likes	Dislikes
Facebook							
Linkedin							
Youtube							
Instagram							
Twitter							
Total							
YTD Stats	Posts	Views	Downloads	Followers	Shares	Likes	Dislikes
Facebook							
Linkedin							
Youtube							
Instagram							
Twitter							
Total							

Work Sheet 2.2 Social media presence

Presentation Notes and Formats

Tables, bar graphs, or both, comparing current YTD to previous YTD.

KPI: Number and Value of Online Share of Voice (OSOV)

Owner	Social Media Manager or Communications Department
Data Sources and Collection	There is a lot to cover here. My recommendation is that the basic data collection be outsourced to a monitoring service. An SEO company may assist here. There are also companies that can monitor mentions for your center and your competitors. The search for "mentions" is much easier in the digital world than using old-fashioned "clipping services." It is also less expensive. To obtain more in-depth analysis, your Social Media Manager or communications staff should handle that task separately.
Reporting Frequency	Quarterly

Why This KPI Is Useful

OSOV is the share of "mentions" about your convention center compared to competitors. For this KPI, OSOV is a "mention" originated by sources other than your own social media presence. The source of mentions comes from online versions of the many magazines that cover our industry, from blogs, online versions of newspapers, and of course social media. Depending on the level of monitoring service ordered, the mentioned content can be identified by source as well as the mentions's sentiment and tone. This enables you to characterize mentions as favorable, unfavorable, or neutral. In order to make the KPI more meaningful, a value can be assigned to the content of the message. For example, favorable content about customer service or food quality is much more valuable than a comment about the convenient walking distance from a hotel to the convention center. Additionally, the source publication that carries the "mention" is of prime importance. A mention in *The Wall Street*

Journal carries more weight than most publications due to circulation and readership, but also because of the publication's stature.

This KPI should be regarded as a principal means for tracking brand value. Tracking competitors' OSOV is also valuable because competitive ranking is always a sign of business performance. Senior management and board members will show great interest in this KPI as it develops.

Objective

Obtain valuable marketing information posted in the public domain about your convention center.

Managing Unfavorable Conclusions and Inferences

The worst outcome of OSOV is to have none; your convention center is inconsequential, nothing of any import or interest happens there. Secondary to being ignored is the receipt of bad news. I would say that an OSOV report categorizing most of the mentions as unfavorable in sentiment from high-value sources cannot be ignored. First, your communications team has to respond, especially if the mention is not true, exaggerated or reckless and irresponsible. If the mention is a legitimate complaint, answer it professionally. For a more proactive action, I would review your center's own social media presence. Is your presence scaled properly? Is its content substantive or just fluff? Does it accurately reflect the business and community value of the convention center?

How to Calculate and/or Organize Data

1. Use Work Sheet 2.3 or similar method to compare for your convention center and principal competitors.
2. Establish a qualitative scale for Sentiment and Tone (1 to 5 as the highest where the lower score is highly unfavorable) and record value accordingly on the work sheet column for Sentiment/Tone Value.
3. Establish a qualitative scale for Content Value and Source Publication Value (1 to 3 as the highest) and record values accordingly on the work sheet columns.

4. Sum the three values in items 2 and 3 above to obtain a score for the "mention."

5. Sum all "mentions" scores to obtain YTD Total Score.

CAPITAL CITY CONVENTION CENTER - NUMBER AND VALUE OF OSOV							
Mention Source	Date	Topic/ Headline	Sentiment/ Tone	Sentiment/ Tone Value	Content Value	Source Value	Score
Conferenza	01-Feb-09	Food Prices	Unfav.	1	3	1	5
Twitter	10-Feb-19	Security Screening	Fav.	4	3	1	8
KABC	12-Mar-19	IT Event crowds	Fav.	4	1	3	8
						YTD Total Score	21

Work Sheet 2.3 Number and value of OSOV

Presentation Notes and Formats

Tables for column topics, bar graphs to display Total Score, comparing current YTD to previous YTD.

Things to Watch for—Misinterpretations, Nuances, and Cautions

Make Certain that Exclusive Contractors Promptly Disclose Their Corporate Social Media Postings and OSOV Social Media Mentions: In business as in life you are often judged by the company you keep. If your exclusive contractor is a large company with regional and national accounts and clients, then you need to be well informed of their corporate social media posts and OSOV mentions. As with most large companies, there are often M&A rumors and actions as well as gained or lost business and occasional scandals. A good deal of this news can be misinterpreted and exaggerated, especially bad news. For the most part scandals and unfavorable business news involve an account not associated with your convention center. It's a good practice to be well informed and stay ahead of these issues.

KPI: Justification for Discounting Rent

Owner	Sales Department and the General Manager
Data Sources and Collection	The Sales Department and CVB will provide prospective event statistics. The estimated economic impact will be calculated by using the convention center's economic feasibility study and follow-up research.
Reporting Frequency	Annually

Why This KPI Is Useful

In most cities, there is a sales and marketing policy that identifies Convention and Visitor Bureaus (CVBs) as deal maker for events occurring more than a year out. This occurs for large events (usually with association clients) when the forecast is for attendees (or delegates) to use a certain amount of hotel rooms. An example may be 2,500 rooms or more (considered a "city wide" event) allowing the CVB to negotiate and possibly discount rent and services if needed. Some convention centers report discounting activities in their annual report. The Los Angeles Convention Center (LACC) annual report shows discounts as a deduction to operating revenues. In LACC's 2015 Annual Report, deductions were valued between 35 and 40 percent ($4.62 million) of annual published rent. In Chicago, the Metropolitan Pier and Exposition Authority (MPEA) has an incentive fund (provided by the state of Illinois), which reimburses up to $15 million per year to MPEA for incentives (discounts) offered to event organizers to bring events to McCormick Place. Their financial statement of rent revenue includes projected receipts from the MPEA Incentive Fund based on events currently contracted. One can hardly call incentives paid by state taxes to cover rent and service discounts as earned revenue. The incentive is a subsidy. The $15 million cap or allowance is estimated at more than 40 percent of McCormick Place's 2019 forecasted rent revenues. These two examples of discounts, LACC and McCormick Place, applied in order to obtain events are not minor but rather material losses of revenue. Fortunately, the situation is slowly changing nationally as convention centers can no longer afford to discount rent heavily or at all.

Discounting space rent can always be justified; the economic impact of an event's direct spending is always greater than the loss of rental income. The scale of economic impact is multiplied substantially when indirect and induced spending are added. But in the practical world of business this logic is out of place. The public and interested taxpayers understand the impact of direct spending. Indirect and induced economic impacts are not easily recognized or understood and adding them without a convincing explanation leads to skepticism. For convention center employees, economic impact seems abstract and remote from their bird's eye view of events. Something more grounded is needed if a center elects to claim the reputation as being well managed. For a convention center, the goal of covering costs and eventually achieving positive cash flow is as satisfying to center management and employees, board members, and political supporters as economic impact is. Favorable income and cash flow statements have these attributes:

- A solid ring of truth; they are real and demonstrate management competence.
- They resonate well with taxpayers and public advocates who are skeptical of large economic impact statistics.
- They add legitimacy, believability, and clarity to economic impact reporting.

Objective

Five years ago it was my opinion that discounting rent occurred too often and too easily. This was based on conversations with event organizers who rarely found negotiating rent concessions and discounts very challenging. They always got what they wanted, often with just a phone call. This KPI will force what I believe to be necessary accountability for convention center and CVB sales teams alike. Discounting rent occurs much less now but the legacy of "convention centers are loss leaders and not designed to make a profit" still survives, sending a wrong message to sales teams. Many cities have gone to contractual agreements with CVBs, which formalize booking policies as well as setting limits and controls with the ultimate approval of deals by the convention centers. The agreement between the San Diego Convention Center (SDCC) and the San Diego CVB (now San Diego Tourism) is an excellent example. In that agreement the SDCC also pays the CVB an annual fee for sales and marketing services. If this KPI is implemented as this process matures, center management will train their sales team and become more engaged in the review process and challenge CVB methods when discounts are applied too liberally.

Managing Unfavorable Conclusions and Inferences

When the sum of discounts for rent and services is reviewed annually and deemed too high, there is cause to develop a more disciplined negotiating strategy. Focus on obtaining as much business intelligence as possible in order to assess an event organizer's real intentions. This means that sales teams will need to understand the business behavior of prospects. They should look at the event's history; contact venues where the event played previously, consult hoteliers, general service contractors, and other trustworthy parties. Look for "tells." I have been in this situation many times before. In one instance I was involved in a very active negotiation for a major tradeshow. The event organizer negotiated aggressively. Then, through a random conversation with a printing company that both the Javits Center and the event organizer used, we learned that marketing material for the event was already printed and distributed to prospective exhibiting companies, identifying the Javits Center as the location for the event. When others on Javits staff engaged in conversation about planning with the event organizer's operations team, there were more and more small indications that their intention was to locate the event at the Javits Center. We found no cause to discount rent.

How to Calculate and/or Organize Data

Compose and maintain a work sheet similar to Work Sheet 2.4:

JUSTIFICATION AND RECORD FOR DISCOUNTING SPACE RENT					
Event	Dates	Rent	Proposed Rent	Justification for Discount	Validation of Exhibitors and Attendees
State Music Teachers Convention	May 30-June 1	52,500	36,750	Necessary to close deal. Discount and successful event will lead to futu re bookings.Attendance 2,800	Pre event numbers are valid to 1%
Rocky Mountain Mining Asso. Annual Meeting	Oct. 11-13	71,400	42,840	Competed with Denver (CCC) which offered no rent. Attendance 3,180	Attendance was 2987, confirmed by CVB

Work Sheet 2.4 Justification and record for discounting rent

Presentation Notes and Formats

Table with General Manager and head of sales commentary.

CHAPTER 3

Earned (or Operating) Service Revenue Details: Derivatives

KPI: Comparing Targeted Market Profitability and Profit per GSF Rented to Other (Non - Targeted Market) Events

Owner	Event Operations Department
Data Sources and Collection	The Finance Department will have all the earned revenue and profit or loss for all events. The Sales Department will provide information about all events, both targeted market and non-targeted market events and the GSF Rented.
Reporting Frequency	Annually

Why This KPI Is Useful

For convention centers in top tier cities it is presumed that their targeted market are events that draw the most out-of-town attendees and are the most profitable. It's useful to affirm that targeted events meet or exceed those expectations. For lower tiered cities the targeted markets may be the events that have the highest probability of locating in your city.

It's a good management practice to know as much as you can about how targeted markets spend on event services. As the KPI title implies, when the KPI is implemented, after a time you will have unique data-based knowledge of the event spending history for targeted economic sectors. This information will enable your management team to sell effectively, to price services smartly, to plan event move in installation more efficiently, and to forecast event revenues more accurately. In my time at the Javits Center, we had a separate database of all billable items (numbers and revenues) by service category. We did not link this database to Excel spreadsheets. Rather, we took billable item data and event type and economic sector information and manually calculated business metrics. For example, if the sales team said they had a prospect in the targeted economic sector, like Technology we could estimate the mix of billable items and the revenue per NSF for that prospect.

Objective

Obtain a unique knowledge base of targeted market profitability and how it compares with other business not targeted.

Managing Unfavorable Conclusions and Inferences

This KPI may be considered unfavorable if data results do not meet expectations. If revenue and profit expectations were high for a certain targeted market, but results are much less, review the rationale behind the current target market selection with the CVB.

How to Calculate and/or Organize Data

Use Work Sheet 3.1and 3.1a to organize and calculate the differences between targeted and the non-targeted market events.

PROFITABILITY OF TARGETED MARKRT VS. NON-TARGETED MARKET EVENTS			
	Targeted Market	Non -Targeted Market	All Events
# of Events	50	115	165
Earned Revenue	5,494,205	7,905,895	13,400,100
Profit Margin	5.8%	1.4%	3.2%
Profit	318,664	110,552	429,216
Ave. Profit/Event	$6,374	$957	$2,601

Work Sheet 3.1 Profitability of targeted market vs. non-targeted market events

PROFIT/GSF RENTED OF TARGETED MARKRT VS. NON-TARGETED MARKET EVENTS			
	Targeted Market	Non -Targeted Market	All Events
GSF Rented	2,480,000	1,380,000	3,860,000
Profit	318,664	110,552	429,216
Profit/KGSF	$0.128	$0.080	$0.11

Work Sheet 3.1a Profit/ GSF Rented of targeted market vs. non-targeted market events

Presentation Notes and Formats

Table, bar graph, or both, comparing current YTD to previous YTD.

KPI: Utility Service Labor Hours per Billable Item

Owner	Event Operations Department
Data Sources and Collection	The Finance Department will have this data. If the "KPI: Operating Profit or Loss Statements for Each Event" is used and its work sheets completed, then through linking spreadsheets using MS Excel, this KPI can be automatically updated very soon after each event.
Reporting Fre-quency	Monthly or more frequently if data are collected by linking spreadsheets per the above.

Why This KPI Is Useful

Services are generally referred to as "orders." However, in each order there can be several billable items, for example, for electric—208 V, three-phase supply, 20 A service; 1500 W outlet; display lights; an extension cord, and so on. An exhibitor then will request one or several billable items in their order. Some billable items are easy to install and are lower priced, whereas others are more time consuming and rely on special skills and equipment to render service.

Along with examining productivity in terms of dollars, it is necessary to track how long it takes to fulfill each billable item. This step is necessary because the message of higher productivity will ultimately fall on show floor supervision and electricians and plumbers. They think in terms of labor hours and will better understand the objective.

Center management should intuitively know by observation whether there is potential for higher productivity. You may see workers who are not well organized with tools and materials, workers who socialize too much, workers who appear untrained, and those who are simply too slow. Measuring Labor Hours per Billable Item is a building block to set productivity goals and assess the competency of show floor supervision.

Objective

Labor hours have more meaning to supervisors and rank-and-file workers. The objective is the same—increase labor productivity.

Managing Unfavorable Conclusions and Inferences

As with most unfavorable productivity metrics, review and discuss work routines with supervisors, apply reasonable times, and set specific objectives for upcoming events. You may learn of material and supply problems or a lack of coordination with other trades working on exhibit booths. Supervisors must know that they are accountable for satisfactory results for task completions such as how many electric orders filled in a given time.

How to Calculate and/or Organize Data

1. Sum electric and plumbing labor hours separately.
2. Sum electric and plumbing service billable items separately.
3. Divide labor hours by billable items to obtain the labor hours per billable item.

Presentation Notes and Formats

Table, line graph, or both, comparing current YTD to previous YTD and plan,

KPI: Percentage of Utility Service Order Fulfillment Before the Last Move in Day

Owner	Event Operations Department
Data Sources and Collection	The Event Operations Department will record and provide order fulfillment percentages.
Reporting Frequency	Monthly

Why This KPI Is Useful

Productivity of the workforce will improve if utility service orders can be completed before freight arrival, the start of intensive building, and the arrival of exhibiting company staff. Additionally, the exhibiting companies need time to prepare their products and sales presentations, so orders fulfilled before the last day of move in are very important. In my time at the Javits Center, this KPI worked extremely well. Supervisors and electricians were very conscious of the KPI's importance. For us, the order fulfillment objective caused profit margins to increase noticeably. Sometime certain KPIs hit a positive chord with the workforce and management should be mindful of this.

Objective

Order fulfillment should be at least 85 percent before the last move-in day.

Managing Unfavorable Conclusions and Inferences

Unfavorable results in this KPI have three probable causes: poor production planning by the GSC, an inordinate amount of late (floor) orders from exhibitors, or poor labor productivity. Two of them can be solved by more attentive management and detailed production planning with the GSC.

How to Calculate and/or Organize Data

1. Sum all utility orders (separate electric and plumbing).
2. Divide total utility orders completed before the second to the last day of event move in by total utility orders for the event to obtain the percentage of order fulfillment.

Presentation Notes and Formats

Table with line or bar graph, comparing current YTD to previous YTD and plan. Figure 3.1 and 3.1a are samples of bar graph presentations.

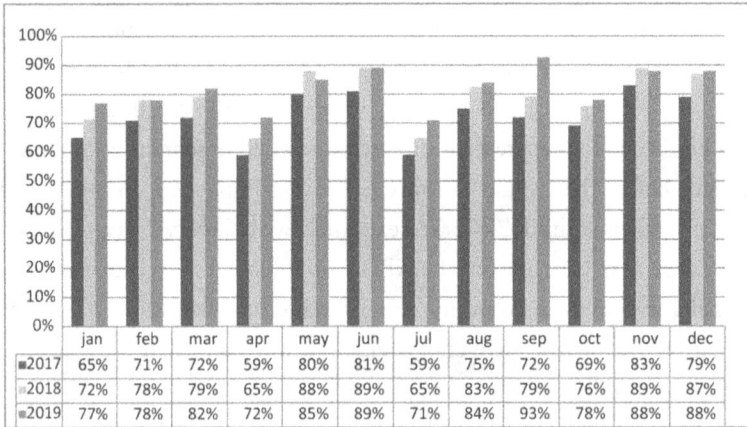

	jan	feb	mar	apr	may	jun	jul	aug	sep	oct	nov	dec
2017	65%	71%	72%	59%	80%	81%	59%	75%	72%	69%	83%	79%
2018	72%	78%	79%	65%	88%	89%	65%	83%	79%	76%	89%	87%
2019	77%	78%	82%	72%	85%	89%	71%	84%	93%	78%	88%	88%

Figure 3.1 Utility order fulfillment by month - before the last move - in day

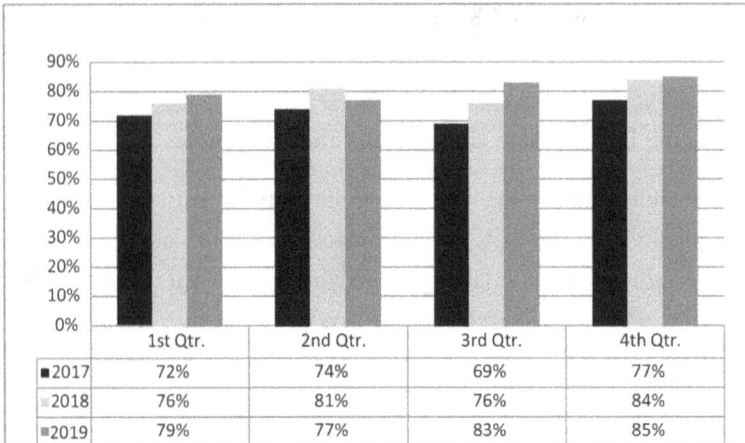

	1st Qtr.	2nd Qtr.	3rd Qtr.	4th Qtr.
2017	72%	74%	69%	77%
2018	76%	81%	76%	84%
2019	79%	77%	83%	85%

Figure 3.1a Utility order fulfillment by quarter - before the last move - in day

Figure 3.1 is an "eyeful" with too much compressed information, making this graphic unsuitable for a presentation. As Figure 3.1a shows, a simple remedy is to lessen the time intervals of the x-axis to quarters rather than months.

KPI: Application of Electric Service Productivity KPIs to Individual Exhibit Halls

Owner	Event Operations Department
Data Sources and Collection	The Event Operations Department will have to separate the labor hours and the exhibit booth numbers for each exhibit hall. This can be done progressively after each event for the month. Average productivity for all exhibit halls should also be calculated and recorded.
Reporting Frequency	Monthly

Why This KPI Is Useful

In many convention centers, a supervisor is assigned to be in charge of utility installations and dismantling for each exhibit hall. It is their competency in planning, coordinating with other contractors, dealing with exhibitors, and supervising electricians that drives profit. In my experience, consistently poor performers were replaced and this nearly always provided improved performance. This KPI measures the following productivity KPIs for individual exhibit halls:

- Utility Services (Electric only) Profit or Commissions/NSF. If this KPI is below average, then proceed with the KPIs below.
- Utility Service (Electric only) Labor Hours per Billable Item
- Percentage of Electric Service Order Fulfillment Before the Last Move in Day

Objective

Hold floor supervision accountable for utility service productivity.

Managing Unfavorable Conclusions and Inferences

This KPI is too important for trials and extra training. If a supervisor is clearly not suited for this job and cannot consistently meet or exceed business objectives, they should be replaced.

How to Calculate and/or Organize Data

1. Sort and organize data by exhibit hall.
2. Calculate the productivity KPIs listed above for each exhibit hall.
3. Calculate the average productivity for the KPIs and compare to individual exhibit halls.

Presentation Notes and Formats

Tables for each KPI and each exhibit hall, line graphs, or both, comparing current YTD, previous YTD, and business plan averages vs. individual performance.

Things to Watch for—Misinterpretations, Nuances, and Cautions

KPI Reports Should, By Footnote, Record Discounts and Package Deals: These circumstances occur from time to time as a price concession, for single payers, like show management or a corporate sponsor, who pay in advance for high-volume services, which are the same for each exhibit booth or selected exhibitors. As an example, this typically happens for electric service if each exhibit booth has the exact same display lighting.

Food and Beverage (F and B)

KPI: Gross Revenues and Profit Margins (in %) for Each Category of F and B Service

Owner	F and B contractor and whichever convention center department administers the contract.
Data Sources and Collection	The F and B contractor is the source of data. Nearly all F and B contractors have a point-of-sale system used in restaurants, concessions, and carts, which can easily be programmed to provide the necessary statistics.
Reporting Frequency	Annually

Why This KPI Is Useful

Margins vary on type of service and also type of products sold, particularly alcoholic beverages. Types of service are; restaurant/concession, booth catering, meeting room catering and banquets, vending machines, and other. It's good management practice to know how your contractor does business. Also, it's useful for Sales to know which category is the most profitable. In most centers, the most profitable service category is large banquets.

Objective

Obtain a knowledge base on which category of F and B service provides the greater profit margin.

Managing Unfavorable Conclusions and Inferences

Not applicable.

How to Calculate and/or Organize Data

Recommend using a similar work sheet to Work Sheet 3.2:

F AND B GROSS REVENUE AND PROFIT MARGIN FOR EACH SERVICE CATEGORY								
	THIS YEAR – 2019				PREVIOUS YEAR – 2018			
Service Category	Gross Revenue	% of Total Revenues	Profit Margin	Comm. %	Gross Revenue	% of Total Revenues	Profit Margin	Comm. %
Restaurants/ Concessions								
Catering-Meeting Rooms								
Catering – Ballroom								
Exhibit Booth Catering								
Vending Machines								
Other								
Total								

Work Sheet 3.2 F and B gross revenue and profit margin for each service category

Presentation Notes and Formats

Table, bar graph, or both, comparing current year to previous year(s).

KPI: Average Number of Checks (aka Receipts) and Check Price per Event Type and Economic Sector in Restaurants and Concessions

Owner	F and B contractor and whichever convention center department administers the contract.
Data Sources and Collection	The F and B contractor is the source of data. Nearly all F and B contractors have a point-of-sale system in restaurants, concessions, and carts, which can easily be programmed to accumulate this data.
Reporting Frequency	Annually

Why This KPI Is Useful

Attendees at each event type and economic sector have different spending habits. This KPI will show the average number of checks or receipts issued and the average price per check. It's good to know the on-site spending habits for F and B by event type and economic sector. When compared to overall attendance the data will show what percentage of the exhibitors and attendees have meals at the event and more (day, time of day, etc.). Drilled down further, the data will show preferences for type of food and beverage for each event type and economic sector.

Objective

Obtain a knowledge base on the business volume and value of restaurants and concessions per event type and economic sector.

Managing Unfavorable Conclusions and Inferences

Not applicable.

How to Calculate and/or Organize Data

Recommend using a work sheet similar to Work Sheet 3.3:

F AND B AVERAGE NUMBER OF CHECKS AND CHECK PRICE PER EVENT TYPE			
Type of Event	**Ave. Number of Checks**	**Ave. Check Price**	**Remarks**
Consumer Show			
Tradeshow			
Conventions w/exhibits			
Sports			
Entertainment			
Other			
Overall Aveerage			
F AND B AVERAGE NUMBER OF CHECKS AND CHECK PRICE PER EVENT SECTOR			
Event Economic Sector	**Ave. Number of Checks**	**Ave. Check Price**	**Remarks**
Consumer Goods			
Tech			
Health Science			
Manufng. /Industrial			
Fashion			
Food			
Arts.Sports or Leisure			
Entertainment			
Sport Events			
Religion			
Finance			
Other			
Overall Average			

Work Sheet 3.3 Average number and price of checks per event type and economic sector

Presentation Notes and Formats

Table, bar graph, or both, comparing current year to previous year (s).

Communications Service

KPI: Record of Wi-Fi Complaints

Owner	Communications Contractor and whichever convention center department administers the contract.
Data Sources and Collection	The communications contractor is the source of data.
Reporting Frequency	Quarterly

Why This KPI Is Useful

Wi-Fi was first rolled out in the 1990s. It took hold rapidly and is a requisite service in every meeting venue. Based on a networking technology called ethernet, Wi-Fi manufacturers and providers probably never envisioned the popularity of wireless and the explosive growth of mobile devices. The problem with ethernet technology (access points, cabling, routers, and switches) is that it cannot handle concentrated high-volume situations as you may find at a business event. One writer, Isaac Carey, writing in a *Skift* magazine article "Why Is Wi-Fi at Events Still So Bad?" described the problem this way:

> Sluggish internet speeds, a network that suddenly cuts out, and odd corners of the room that somehow have adequate service as long as you hold your phone at a specific angle. These are the problems that nearly every conference attendee, trying in vain to use the provided Wi-Fi, has faced at least once, especially at a large event.[1]

The article goes on to describe the frustration event organizers experience when unreliability of a Wi-Fi system surfaces. Most center managers have

---

[1] Carey, I., October 9, 2019. "Why is WiFi at Events So Bad? " https://skift.com/2019/10/09/why-is-wi-fi-at-events-still-so-bad/ (accessed December, 2019).

had to deal with complaints with no easy answers. An expert and popular lecturer on event technology issues, Corbin Ball, commented on this:

> Convention centers are in a dilemma. Most have spent millions of dollars building and updating their existing Wi-Fi services. Yet the demand for wireless broadband continues to grow. Good broadband is a key factor for many planners in making their venue selections. Centers would like to at least get their investment back before upgrading to newer technology. But, as the demand continues to grow, they will eventually need to invest in technologies that can handle this growth. Wi-Fi6 is a natural (greater speed, more connections, less congestion, and greater security). 5G will be later in the process.[2]

Emerging technology improvements such as Wi-Fi6 or 5G will be prohibitively expensive for some time and there are some who believe the wireless congestion at certain events will never go away. Experienced communications practitioners believe that new technologies will quickly be faced with congestion similar to current Wi-Fi. Bandwidth demands will dramatically increase. As an example, consider the potential growth of 8K video, which projects an image resolution with a width of approximately 8,000 pixels, twice the current standard for large TV screens. Imagine then clusters of exhibitors at a tradeshow looking for 8K service. Couple bandwidth demand growth with more powerful mobile devices and you have a perfect setting for poor service unless a sizable investment is made to upgrade. Corbin Ball believes that "savvy planners will limit their choices to venues with a Wi-Fi infrastructure that will meet their anticipated needs (Wi-Fi has become the lifeblood of event communications!)"

Managing Unfavorable Conclusions and Inferences

This KPI requires precise location mapping and a narrative and technical description of the circumstances leading to the complaint. A quick

---

[2] Ball, C., Expert, Writer and Lecturer on Event Technology, 2020 (January 17), E-mail message to author.

and affordable solution to this problem seems improbable at this time. To solve the problem, you may have to acquiesce and manage the event's Wi-Fi service expectations or if you can afford it, get creative and lease rather than purchase added or new equipment. To gage this, take time to review the actions taken by Consumer Electronics Show (CES) in their 2019 event to provide adequate wireless communications for the largest and most important Tech event worldwide. The CES team added Access Points (APs) in as dense an arrangement as technically possible. Additionally they added several Distributed Antenna Systems (DAS) and Cell on Wheels (COWS) to divert some of the wireless traffic to cells. DAS consists of a network of antennas that offer cellular service for a building area.

How to Calculate and/or Organize Data

See Work Sheet 3.4 as a means of recording complaints:

RECORD OF WiFi COMPLAINTS							
Complaint Number /Code	Location	Event Name	Date	Nature of Complaint	Was Problem Solved? Y/N	How Long Did it Take?	Remarks
1 – 001	Hall A, adjacent to Booth 1250	IT for Edu- cators Expo	Feb. 2, 2019	Internet too slow	N	NA	Too much mobile- phone traffic for AP
2 – 003	Main Ballroom	Tech Expo	Mar 12, 2019	Internet stopped working	Y	17 m	Occurred during Keynote speech, switch problem

Work Sheet 3.4 Record of WiFi complaints

Presentation Notes and Formats

Table, bar graph, or both comparing current YTD and several past YTD of complaints. Additionally, a graphic or map is needed of the floor plan for each exhibit hall and other space like ballrooms and large meeting spaces showing the location of APs. The complaint location should be marked with an icon (for each event perhaps color-coded to indicate severity or type of complaint and a footnote where complaints are briefly described in a legend format). Regard the mapping graphic as a working document, shared with event organizers and used for wireless communications planning.

Cleaning

KPI: Cleaning Labor Hours per GSF Rented, NSF, and Total Carpeted Area

Owner	Event Operations Department
Data Sources and Collection	The Finance Department will provide event labor hours data. Sales will provide GSF and NSF data. Event Operations will provide Total Carpeted Area square footage.
Reporting Frequency	Monthly

Why This KPI Is Useful

Along with examining productivity in terms of dollars, it is necessary to track how long it takes to fulfill each cleaning order. This step is necessary because the message of higher productivity will ultimately fall on show floor supervision and the cleaners. They think in terms of labor hours and will better understand the objective. Center management should intuitively know by observation whether there is potential for higher productivity. You may see workers who socialize too much, workers who appear untrained, and those who are simply too slow. Measuring Labor Hours per GSF, NSF, and Total Carpeted Area square footage is the building block to set productivity goals and assess the competency of show floor supervision. Labor is by far the biggest cost factor in calculating profit for cleaning services. Expressing labor productivity in terms of hours per area to be cleaned is a more effective and actionable indicator.

Objective

Labor hours have more meaning to supervisors and rank-and-file workers. The objective is the same—increase labor productivity.

Managing Unfavorable Conclusions and Inferences

As with most unfavorable productivity metrics, review and discuss work routines with supervisors, apply reasonable times, and set specific objectives for upcoming events. You may learn of material and supply problems or a lack of coordination with other trades working on exhibit booths. Supervisors must know that they are accountable for satisfactory results for task completions such as how long it takes to vaccuum 100 square feet.

How to Calculate and/or Organize Data

1. Sum cleaning event labor hours.
2. Sum GSF, NSF, and Total Carpeted Area square footage separately.
3. Divide labor hours by GSF, NSF, and Total Carpeted Area square footage to obtain the labor hours/GSF, NSF, and Total Carpeted Area square footage.

Presentation Notes and Formats

Table, line graph, or both, comparing current YTD, previous YTD and business plan.

KPI: Cleaning Profit /GSF Rented, NSF, and Total Carpeted Area for Each Event Type and Economic Sector

Owner	Event Operations Department
Data Sources and Collection	The Finance Department will provide all financial data. The Sales Department will provide GSF and NSF data and categorize events by type and economic sector. The Event Operations Department will provide total carpeted area square footage and waste haul cost estimates for each event.
Reporting Frequency	Annually

Why This KPI Is Useful

This indicator is a productivity measure showing the different financial results for event types and economic sectors. This KPI includes profit applied to all cleaning services; "trash out", waste hauls, and carpet vaccuuming. It will also make forecasting more accurate for event types and economic sectors.

Objective

Obtain a knowledge base for which event types and economic sectors are the most profitable for cleaning services.

Managing Unfavorable Conclusions and Inferences

The explanation is the same as KPI: Cleaning Labor Hours per GSF Rented, NSF and Total Carpeted Area.

How to Calculate and/or Organize Data

1. Sum all cleaning revenues (incl. Trash out) or commissions for each event type and economic sector. Note that waste hauls are another element of cleaning revenues but are usually not part of an exclusive cleaning contractors work. Waste hauling services are transacted by the center with a separate contractor. The sum of waste haul invoices to the event organizer should be subtracted from the cost of waste hauling to obtain profit for each event type and economic sector. When multiple events are playing simultaneously the waste haul revenue and profit will have to be estimated for each event.
2. If cleaning service is "in – house" subtract cleaning expenses for each event type and economic sector to obtain profit for carpet vacuuming and trash out.
3. Add waste haul profit to commissions or in-house profit for carpet vacuuming and trash out.
4. Sum Total Carpeted Area square footage for each event for carpet vacuuming and trash out type and economic sector
5. For each event type and economic sector, divide profit or commissions by total carpeted area to obtain Cleaning Profit/ Total Carpeted Area for Each Event Type and Economic Sector.

Presentation Notes and Formats

This format will have to be rich with data as it covers multiple event types and economic sectors all organized to show comparisons and results over time. Begin with tables organized where the best performers are on top and the rest are then listed below in descending order. Bar graphs will work also as annual statistics are compared.

Other Earned Revenue Sources

KPI: Amount and Percentage of Individual Revenue Generating Activities Categorized as "Other"

Owner	Event Operations Department
Data Sources and Collection	The Finance Department will provide all data
Reporting Frequency	Annually

Why This KPI Is Useful

Tracking which "other" earned revenue source will show which one has potential for growth. At some point the better ones will be reviewed in the same fashion as the principal earned revenue source.

The "Other" is a category that includes many smaller earned revenue sources. Together they contribute to profit or may be an offset to operating expenses. Listed below are some examples:

- *Profits or Commissions from Audio/Visual services*: Audio/ Visual services is normally outsourced to a professional AV company. Their business arrangement with convention centers is likely to be "official" or "preferred" rather than "exclusive." They pay commissions to the convention center based on gross sales.
- *Charges for Unscheduled Changes in Meeting Room and Ballroom Furniture Setups* (tables, chairs, risers, podiums, etc.):

Most convention centers include furniture setups for meeting room and ballroom activities in the space rent. Unscheduled changes after the setup is put in place are normally charged on a per piece or time and material basis.

- *Overhead Rigging*: Many convention centers are beginning to require that all overhead rigging (signs, banners, display components, AV equipment, etc.) be installed and dismantled by in-house trades. This has developed for consistent safety measures by trained workers and to improve the poor cleanup and conditions contractors leave in the overhead rigging points and structure when the event ends.

- *On-site Advertising and Sponsorship Revenue*: This profit center consists of on-site signage and the use of other media owned and operated by the convention center such as backlit signage and large and small LED screens. Typical advertising and sponsorship clients include hotels, restaurants, and occasionally local and regional banks and major employers. Larger convention centers may have national corporate sponsors such as credit card companies and automobiles. This profit center can advance from modest to major if ad and sponsorship sales are pursued thoughtfully and actively. Additionally, there are a growing number of centers that have sold naming rights. The latest is Cobo Hall in Detroit, which sold naming rights to Chemical Bank for $33 million over a 22-year term ($1.5 million per year).

- *Event Security Services*: There are a few convention centers that have event security as an exclusive service. Others offer the service but compete with other security companies.

- *Transportation Services*: This consists mostly of airport van and private car services. It is not an exclusive service.

- *On-site Retail*: Convenience and sundry stores, business technology stores selling mobile devices and accessories, and city souvenir stores selling popular local branded items from city attractions, sports teams, and others are popular on-site retail stores. Revenue is normally commission based on gross revenue with a minimum guarantee.

- *Medical Services*: Medical teams consisting of nurses, EMTs and certain equipment such as ambulances are normally supplied by the convention center for events.

Objective

Track and compare growth of new earned revenue sources.

Managing Unfavorable Conclusions and Inferences

Not applicable until enough data has been collected in order to set objectives.

How to Calculate and/or Organize Data

1. Sum revenues for each earned revenue source.
2. Sum all to obtain total Other Earned Revenue.
3. Divide each separate earned revenue source by total of Other Earned Revenue to obtain the percentage of each to total Other Earned Revenue.

Presentation Notes and Formats

Tables showing revenue amounts and percentages of total for current year, previous year, and plan. Table 3.1 and Figure 3.2 show a sample of a table and a segmented ring chart describing the "other" earned revenue categories.

GROWTH OF "OTHER" EARNED REVENUE CATEGORIES - 2017 – 2019					
	2017	2018	% Change	2019	% Change
Advertising and Sponsorships	1,313,200	1,562,708	19.0%	1,960,000	25.4%
Audio Visual	680,225	700,632	3.0%	747,500	6.7%
Overhead Rigging	487,965	502,604	3.0%	650,620	29.4%
On -site Retail	375,250	379,003	1.0%	395,000	4.2%
Unsched Set - up Changes	80,799	81,607	1.0%	90,785	11.2%
Security Services	21,488	24,711	15.0%	85,950	247.8%
Totals	2,960,943	3,253,281	9.9%	3,929,855	20.8%

Table 3.1 Growth of "other" earned revenue categories – 2017 – 2019

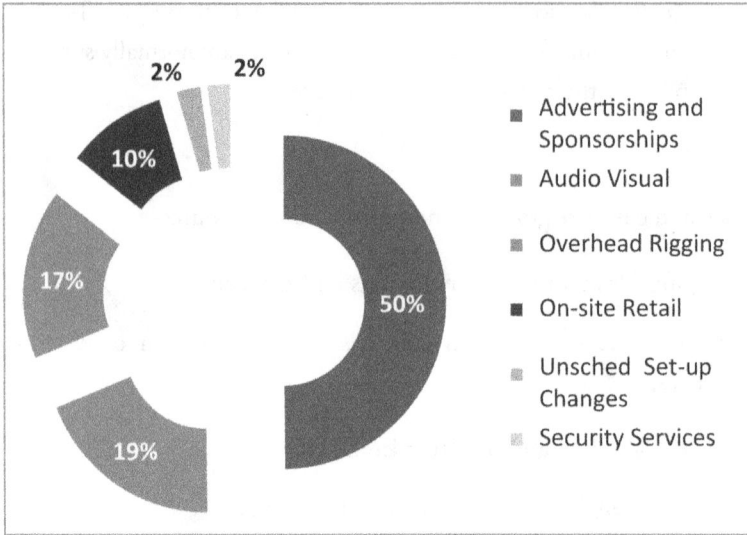

Figure 3.2 2019 Percentage of "other" earned revenue

CHAPTER 4

Operating Expense Details: Derivatives

KPI: Overhead Expenses per GSF Rented

Owner	Finance Department
Data Sources and Collection	The Finance Department will provide all data.
Reporting Frequency	Semi-annually

Why This KPI Is Useful

This KPI applies particularly to revenue models where most of the earned revenue from services is from in-house business units (utility service, parking, cleaning, and so on). I have read and studied well over 20 annual financial and audited financial reports from major U.S., convention centers and the word "overhead" is absent. This is so because overhead expenses at convention centers are semi-variable. Investopedia explains semi-variable overhead expenses as "the company incurs some portion of the expense no matter what, and the other portion depends on the level of business activity."[1] Also, convention centers rarely if ever allocate overhead costs internally to revenue producing activities. So, expenses like utilities, insurance, or even office supplies are not assigned to event service departments. The best way to see the effect of semi-variable overhead expenses is to calculate them on the basis of business activity. In this case business activity is GSF Rented.

---

[1] Investopedia. undated. "Overhead." https://investopedia.com/terms/o/overhead.asp (accessed December 2019).

This KPI explains and enumerates the extent and range overhead expenses vary based on business activity. This metric will assist in exposing irregular increases and patterns of current Overhead Expenses/GSF Rented vs. the average Overhead Expenses/GSF Rented.

Objective

To gain an understanding of overhead costs and how they vary based on business activity.

Managing Unfavorable Conclusions and Inferences

The assumption is that overhead cost may trend at a lower rate of increase than business volume increases. An inordinate increase of overhead expenses per GSF Rented is cause for concern.

How to Calculate and/or Organize Data

1. Sum all direct costs for event services (labor, materials and rented equipment, and field supervision).
2. Subtract the sum of item 1 above from total operating expenses to find overhead costs.
3. Divide overhead costs by GSF.

Presentation Notes and Formats

Table, bar graph, or both, comparing current and current average YTD, previous YTD, and business plan.

CHAPTER 5

KPIs Applied: The Case of the Declining Profit Margin

Business Environment

The Capital City Convention Center has been in operation for six and half years. Their business model is robust with in-house profit centers for utility services, parking, and cleaning. Communications services and food and beverage were awarded as long-term exclusive contracts to leading companies. They also launched a corporate sponsorship program in 2018. In late 2014, the center launched a limited KPI program with plans to expand it as the program matured and proved itself. The center has gradually progressed toward becoming cash flow positive, which was and is a cornerstone of their business strategy. The strategy is enthusiastically supported by the board of directors and the city government.

At the end of 2017, the center achieved positive cash flow. Annual earned revenue was $13.1 million and exceeded annual expenses by $928.8 thousand. In 2018 earned revenue was $13.9 million and exceeded annual expenses by $1.57 million (see Table 5.1). A $2 million goal was attainable. For 2019 the business forecast was favorable; the number of events and occupancy rate were slightly better than 2018. Overall earned revenue, which included rent, utility services, F and B commissions, and parking revenue were all better than 2018. There was growing confidence that by the end of 2019 their cash position will be such that a capital reserve fund can be established. How did they get to this point?

1. By 2015, they found and nurtured several large events, which decided to return each year.
2. In 2016, they implemented a KPI for "Market Pricing Comparisons to Competing Venues" for all parts of their revenue-producing departments. Their main focus was on utility services, which contributed over 30 percent of earned service revenue (see Figure 5.1). The center's pricing was found to be below the average. In 2017 they scrapped their "cost plus" model and event service raised prices to market averages.

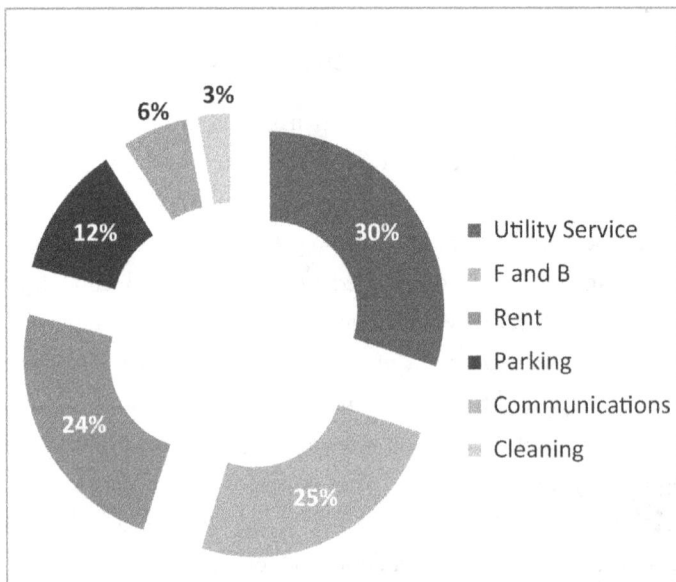

Figure 5.1 Earned revenue percentages (2018)

The Problem

There were signs earlier, but the problem never really took hold until 2019 first quarter review of KPIs. Utility service profits were behind plan and profit/NSF and profit margin had both decreased dramatically—nearly 150% (see Table 5.1). There were some signs in the Monthly Financial Report but not so much as to cause alarm. Most of the 1st quarter losses were attributable to a decline in utility service profit/NSF.

\multicolumn{8}{c}{EARNED REVENUE, PROFIT MARGIN PROFIT PER NSF}							
Year	Earned Revenue	Expenses	Profit	Profit Margin	GSF Rented	NSF	Profit/ NSF
2013	9,460,500	10,965,000	-1,504,500	-15.9%	4,500,000	1,575,000	-1.047
2014	9,447,480	10,840,000	-1,392,520	-14.7%	4,580,000	1,694,600	-1.217
2015	9,774,000	10,440,500	-666,500	-6.8%	4,600,000	1,702,000	-2.554
2016	11,399,000	11,890,500	-491,500	-4.3%	4,775,000	1,805,500	-3.673
2017	13,099,690	12,170,900	928,790	7.1%	4,870,500	1,850,790	1.993
2018	13,923,000	12,350,900	1,572,100	11.3%	4,900,000	1,862,000	1.184
2019 1st Qtr.	3,190,000	3,355,050	-165,050	-5.2%	1,470,000	543,900	-3.295

Table 5.1 Earned revenue profit margin and profit/NSF

The second quarter was already underway. Management resolved to get to the bottom of the problem and fix things quickly. An analysis was put together to examine the worst-possible outcome should the continued decline in utility profit/NSF continue. The idea of reaching $2 million in positive cash flow was at risk. A rough analysis showed that if utility service profit/NSF satyed the same that a possible loss of nearly $500,000 was possible. See Table 5.2 below:

\multicolumn{4}{c}{EFFECT OF CURRENT 2019 UTILITY PRFIT OR LOSS/NSF - END OF 2ND QTR.}			
	Profit	NSF (Actual)	Profit/NSF
2019 1st Qtr. Actual	-165,050	1,575,000	-0.10
2019 1st Qtr. Plan	140,000	1,500,200	0.15
2019 YTD Difference from Plan	-305,050		
\multicolumn{4}{c}{EFFECT OF CURRENT 2019 UTILITY PROFIT/NSF - 2019 YEAR END}			
	Profit	NSF (est.)	Profit/NSF
2019- with Actual 1st Qtr. 2019 Profit/NSF	-204,348	1,950,000	-0.10
2019- Annual Plan	292,500	1,950,000	0.15
2019 Possible Loss	($496,848)		

Table 5.2 Effects of current utility profit or loss/NSF for full year

The Cause

How did the drop in productivity happen? There was more than one cause.

1. Event utility services are led by a head supervisor and a supervisor for each exhibit hall. There are five large exhibit halls. Supervisors are responsible for utility installations. In December 2018, one supervisor retired and another took a lengthy sick leave. The replacements were skilled journeymen who had worked at the convention center for more than a year. By February it became clear that both of the replacement supervisor's productivity metrics were far below average. The manager and the head supervisor should have seen the problem developing in January and taken corrective action.

2. A new General Service Contractor (GSC) entered the market in late 2018 and quickly persuaded a major fraction of event organizers to contract with them. At first, the new GSC was highly disorganized. They had no production plan and failed to consider contractors and labor of different trades coordinating work schedules. The consequence was that electricians and plumbers were unable to follow set routines of laying and dropping utility lines before freight delivery and exhibit building. This occurred four times on major events starting in January up to early February. At the end of February management reviewed the KPI for "Utility Order Fulfillment" for January and February. This KPI was normally calculated quarterly. The fulfillment objective was to complete 85 percent of all service orders before the last move in day. The logic is that utility work flowed unencumbered at a good pace when the floor was not crowded with exhibitors. The first quarter fulfillment rate was 64 percent, accounting for more than half of the loss as shown in figure 5.2.

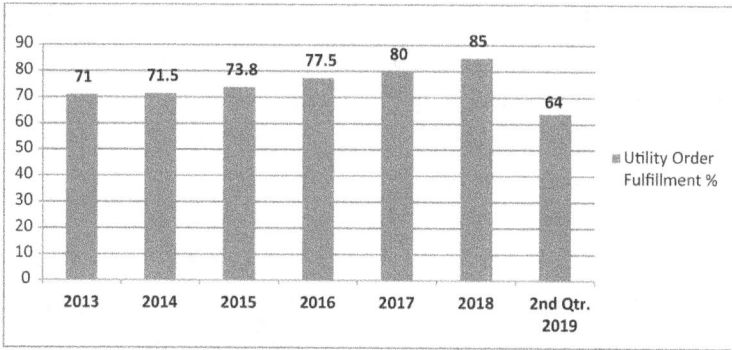

Figure 5.2 Utility order fulfillment

3. In March, a major ice storm delayed the move out of a large event, which was to be immediately followed by the move in of a major consumer show. That move in was to occur on a Friday. Work was unable to begin until very late Friday night through Saturday morning. The show opened on time Saturday morning. However, the labor call had to be increased by 30 percent and the work was all on overtime.

Actions Taken

1. Several meetings were held with the new GSC's owners and managers who conceded there were startup problems with their operation. By mid-February move-ins went as planned and utility order fulfillment and profit/NSF began to improve.
2. One of the supervisors was relieved and replaced in mid-February. The other was given a second chance.
3. With two of the principal causes resolved, it was assumed that as a minimum planned utility service profit/NSF ($.15/NSF) would resume and estimates of forecasted NSF would hold. However, in order to make up for the first 1st quarter and part of April losses, utility service profit/NSF would have to increase to $1.30/NSF. Brainstorming meetings were held with all supervisors and selected journeymen to review work procedures. The objective was to find time-saving methods for utility services. Clearly other earned revenue sources would have to step up and increase revenues and profit.

4. The reporting frequency for Utility Service Profit per NSF and Utility Order Fulfillment was changed from quarterly to monthly.

5. New KPIs were launched in the third quarter:
   - Operating Profit/Loss Statements for Each Event
   - Labor Hours per Billable Item (monthly)
   - Utility Service Profit per NSF for each Exhibit Hall (monthly to monitor supervisor performance)

6. Profit/NSF objectives would be set and closely monitored for each upcoming event.

Lessons Learned

1. In launching their KPI program, center management relied on advice seen frequently in business literature, blogs, and magazines to start a program with just a few KPIs, which fulfill the most fundamental business statistics. Management should have gone deeper. Forgoing and delaying KPIs, which apply to major revenue generators like utility services, parking, F and B, or communications service is bad advice. Better advice is to choose many KPIs and put aside initial impressions that a KPI is redundant and unnecessary. At the beginning, you don't know what you don't know. Try the KPIs for a time until you can judge what really matters based on the value of data, not opinions.

2. KPI reporting frequency matters. In this case study, a quarterly review of utility service productivity measures should have been monthly.

3. As experienced in this case study, in our business things can go wrong quickly:
   - Outside contractors hired by event organizers have their own agenda and methods of working. These can easily conflict with the convention centers. In - house event service divisions and GSCs have to develop and cooperate on event production schedules.
   - Hiring supervisors and managers based on strong supervisory experience is essential. A skilled tradesman doesn't always mean they have the talent and drive to be in charge.
   - Managers must pay closer attention. Having a data-rich resource with KPIs is a great advantage, but you have to ask questions, closely observe and appropriately act on KPIs that do not meet plan or simply seem off, no matter how small.

CHAPTER 6

Security and Safety Derivatives

Security

KPI: Number, Nature, and Source of Serious Threats against the Convention Center and Events

Owner	Public Safety Department
Data Sources and Collection	Most of the data will come from law enforcement (federal Fusion Centers, state, and local). If you have a threat surveillance contractor, a good measure will come from them. These organizations generally have surveillance software, which monitors social media, internet traffic from certain websites, blogs, chat rooms, and from government databases like arrest records. Event organizers may have similar methods.
Reporting Frequency	Quarterly

Why This KPI Is Useful

Violent attacks target public venues in similar ways by employing low-grade tactics against large crowds. Since 9/11, most significant attacks have been shootings, explosives, and simple low-tech methods such as driving vehicles into crowds and knife attacks. Low-tech attacks are consistent with low capability individuals driven by extremist philosophy. They tend to move against soft targets, not hardened well-secured facilities. Convention Centers are "soft targets." Soft targets are well described by the International Association of Venue Managers, "Exhibitions and Meetings Safety and Security Initiative—Convention Center Security Guide":

> Soft targets have high asset attractiveness due to ease of access coupled with high crowd concentrations making mass casualty scenarios within the reach of any adversary regardless of skill sets or support networks. Some other common vulnerabilities associated with soft targets; concentrations (mass casualty), open uncontrolled space, high-speed avenues of approach, multiple egress and entry points, underground parking, light rail, limited standoff distance or setback from streets, minimal security and screening, and significant economic and psychological impact, and media coverage.[1]

Ask yourself, does your center's security operation contribute to the overall management of the venue in a pro-active way? Documenting threats in the fashion described in this KPI is a start.

Objective

Record and analyze threats to establish a knowledge base that informs and directs security plans. This is achieved by relying on intelligence networks such as, local police and your area Fusion Centers and/or contracting with threat surveillance and reporting service. Forewarning of threats should trigger a rapid response plan for protective security measures such as screening devices, bomb sniffing dogs, facial recognition capabilities, and armed protective security personnel.

---

[1] International Association of Venue Managers. 2016. "Exhibitions and Meetings Safety and Security Initiative – Convention Center Security Guide (draft)."

Managing Unfavorable Conclusions and Inferences

More threats mean more security involvement. I would sharpen and expand contingency plans for serious threats and step up security training and security drills. Involve local police and engage a protective security firm for advice and on-site operational support.

How to Calculate and/or Organize Data

Record threats using a security threat worksheet. An example is shown below:

SECURITY THREAT RECORD					
Date of Threat	Source	Event Name	Nature of Threat	Action Taken	Outcome
02-Mar-17	Microsoft Security Div.	Game Developers Conference (GDC)	Physical harm to MS employees	Background and photos from threat contractor, SFPD on-site, SF Hotel Security Asso. help	POI did not show. Threat deterred
04-Feb-18	Threat Contractor	Nat'l Hardware Show	Known POI found on sec. cameras- loading dock	Detained by LVPD who found POI inside center loby during move in	POI arrested - outstanding warrants. Threat stopped

Work Sheet 6.1 Security threat record

Presentation Notes and Formats

Table similar to work sheet. This KPI is confidential, distribute to only employees with "need to know" and mark "Confidential."

KPI: Cyber Security Incident Summary

Owner	IT Department
Data Sources and Collection	I am certain all convention centers have security software installed to protect their systems. These services will track and identify some or all of the KPIs required operating safely.
Reporting Frequency	Quarterly

Why This KPI Is Useful

Tracking cyber threats for a public assembly facility is a full-time endeavor. New, not-seen-before cyber threats arise all the time and this requires constant monitoring.

Objective

Prevent disruption or worse to the center's computer network, devices, computer software applications, data, and e-commerce transactions and customer information.

Managing Unfavorable Conclusions and Inferences

Engage a cyber security consultant.

How to Calculate and/or Organize Data

Work Sheet 6.2 is an example of a tracking work sheet:

CYBER SECURITY INCIDENT SUMMARY				
	Number	YTD Ave. Time to Detect	YTD Ave. Time to Resolve	Cause (s)
Major Incidents	1	3h 15m	2 days	Malware, source unknown
Minor Incidents	7	minutes	20m	Virus, Security contractor investigating
Incidents with Customer Impacts	1	1 week	NA	Phony event services ordered by terminated exhibitor employee
Employee Misuse	5	2h 30m	15m	Downloading video games, gambling on –line

Work Sheet 6.2 Cyber security incident summary

For many of these incidents, there will be a detailed technical report also.

Presentation Notes and Format

Table.

KPI: Percentage of Public Safety and Center Employees Receiving Security Training

Owner	Public Safety Department and Human Resources Department
Data Sources and Collection	Human resources will organize training courses and lectures and keep a record of those receiving training. Public Safety will organize all training and drills with first responders.
Reporting Frequency	Annually

Why This KPI Is Useful

Training requirements for Public Safety Officers are: Active Shooter, Bomb Threat, Suspicious Person Recognition, Handling Mass Casualty Incidents, First Aid, and Building Emergencies. Training key center employees who are not part of the Public Safety Department but are in management and supervisory positions or directly involved with events should also receive this training. Some of this training should take place on site with first responder teams. This KPI is a reminder that security is a prime responsibility for convention center management.

Objective

100 percent training fulfillment for Public Safety Officers, 90 percent training fulfillment for other selected center employees.

Managing Unfavorable Conclusions and Inferences

Training requirements for Public Safety Officers including refresher training cannot be compromised. Initiate a comprehensive training program as soon as practical. Putting this off puts your center at risk of not reacting to an incident properly, of legal action if the incident is poorly handled and people injured or worse, and risk of an unfavorable business reputation.

How to Calculate and/or Organize Data

Maintain a basic work sheet of names, type training and dates completed, and then calculate percentages.

Presentation Notes and Format

Tables, bar graph, or both.

Things to Watch for—Misinterpretations, Nuances, and Cautions

An Explanation of "Threat Surveillance and Reporting Service to Forewarn.": Several event companies contract out for threat surveillance and analysis services. These contractors monitor certain websites, blogs, newsletters, message boards, chat rooms, and social media. Their basic method is to use proprietary software and other intelligence sources to search for keywords and phrases and relationships that portend ill intent. They also have access to government security databases and arrest records. Potential threats are transmitted to company security managers in a timely way so that security preparations in reaction to the threat can be organized.

Convention centers tend to rely on their relationships with local police for threat information. Local police in turn have relationships with DHS "Fusion Centers." Fusion Centers are located in nearly all states. These centers are staffed by various federal security agencies as well as local and state police. Their job is to constantly monitor and analyze potential threats and report same to local police. If there is a strong relationship with local police, convention centers are often well "forewarned." However, there are limits to the extent of forewarning. Local police through the fusion centers may not have knowledge regarding a threat to an exhibiting company or to the business sector the event represents. Fusion center surveillance is focused on terrorism and criminals and they may not pick up on threats from an aggressive advocacy group such as PETA or Greenpeace. Few convention centers outsource threat surveillance and analysis in the fashion that event companies do. The Javits Center may be an exception as is the Las Vegas Convention Center (LVCC). At LVCC threats over the internet and social media are searched for, analyzed, and acted upon by in-house security.

A Uniformed Police Presence Is the Best Security Measure: There are many security measures: camera surveillance, threat surveillance, screening for weapons and explosives, bomb sniffing dogs, and so on. None are better than an established uniformed police presence by means of a satellite police station. They have legitimacy, they are visible, they can make arrests, call for immediate assistance, and they are armed.

Safety

KPI: Record of "Near Misses"

Owner	Public Safety Department
Data Sources and Collection	Observations by security personnel, event service managers, and convention center management. This will be difficult to do consistently unless a manager is assigned and "near miss" inspections are regularly conducted during an event move in or move out.
Reporting Frequency	Quarterly

Why This KPI Is Useful

Near misses (aka "close calls") are hazardous, careless work practices, which could cause death or life-changing injury. Some common near misses in our industry are reckless driving by forklift operators, standing on the top cap of a stepladder while building an exhibit, or working on an articulating lift without fall protection. A record of near misses based on the observations of trained workplace safety inspectors is in my view the most effective indicator of a workplace safety.

Objective

Reduce "Near Misses" as much as practical. Continue "near miss" inspections as a regular routine.

Managing Unfavorable Conclusions and Inferences

If the record of near misses grows unabated, presume that a severe injury will occur at some point.

1. Make certain all employees, particularly event services, know and follow the facility's safety regulations and guidelines. Promulgate these

to all event organizers, their exhibitors including Exhibit Appointed Contractors (EACs), and GSCs.

2. For enforcement of in-house or exclusive contractor employees, the only effective method I've experienced is a stern warning first, followed by a personnel action if an individual violates safety rules again (suspension without pay or termination).

3. Regulate GSCs' and EACs' qualification to work on site based on their workplace safety record, Their safety record is based on the number and severity of injuries, and/or workman's compensation insurance Experience Modification Rating (EMR).

How to Calculate and/or Organize Data

EVENT NEAR MISS INSPECTIONS						
Who	Contractor	Date	Where	Event Name	Nature of Near Miss	Action Taken
L. Jones, Teamster	Freeman	Feb. 18	Grand Lobby	MAGIC	Driving too fast while talking on cell	L. Jones removed from building and suspended without pay
TOTAL						
YTD TOTAL						
YTD TOTAL LAST YR.						
YTD NEAR MISSES/EVENT						

Work Sheet 6.3 Event near miss inspections

Presentation Notes and Formats

Table showing numbers and percentages, categorized by Nature of Near Miss.

KPI: Record of Workman's Compensation (WC) Experience Modification Rating (EMR)

Owner	Human Resources Department (or whatever department the Risk Manager reports to)
Data Sources and Collection	Communication between the insurance carrier or broker and the convention center risk manager
Reporting Frequency	Annually

Why This KPI Is Useful

EMR is a number issued annually by the convention center's WC insurance carrier. The number represents the insurance market's estimation of safety risk. The number regulates the amount of premium paid annually for the WC policy. An EMR of 0.85 means that the convention center will pay 85 percent of the benchmark premium average for the industry. Conversely, an EMR of 1.2 means the center will pay 120 percent of the benchmark premium average for the industry. An EMR of 1.0 or greater is cause to take action. Know that even if injuries and claims decrease insurance carriers look at three years' worth of claims history before you can expect EMR to decrease. The likely causes of high EMR and WC premiums are a poor safety record or employees submitting false or exaggerated WC claims.

Objective

An EMR consistently 1.0 or less.

Managing Unfavorable Conclusions and Inferences

Excessive premiums resulting from a high EMR is an expense that is avoidable. Start by taking injuries and workman's compensation claims and claim management seriously. WC insurance pays all medical expenses plus compensates the employee with a major fraction of wages for as long as they are not able to work. If you need help because of rising EMR and costly premiums, your carrier can be a useful asset. Let's say that as a manager you've just been tasked with controlling WC premium growth. Workman's Compensation insurance premiums can increase in a nonlinear fashion if injuries continue to increase. A $150,000 annual premium can easily increase by $15,000 with an EMR of 1.1. If WC claims are not closed and injuries continue to climb, the next year's EMR could well be 1.25. Now premiums are at $206,250. Moreover it may reach a point where the more reputable insurance companies discontinue coverage. The only solution is to review and restart an aggressive workplace safety program and take a serious look at exaggerated and fraudulent claims. In my experience fraud has always played a big part of rising EMRs and premiums.

How to Calculate and/or Organize Data

EMR is calculated by the WC insurance carrier.

Presentation Notes and Formats

Table, bar or line graph and table, comparing current year and the previous 5 years. See Figure 6.1 of this KPI below:

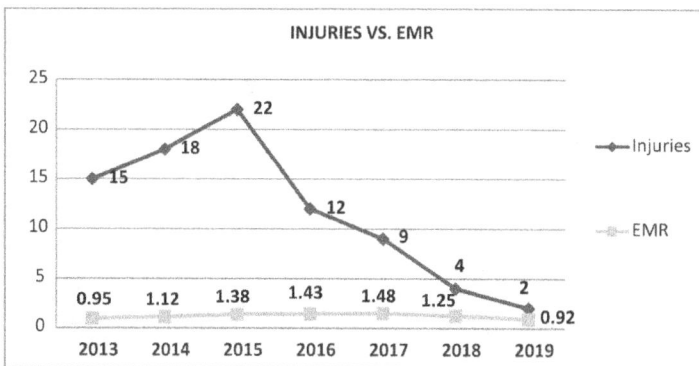

Figure 6.1 History of injuries vs. EMR

Figure 6.1 is a poor example of how to visually depict the relationship between data sets. It is doubtful whether this graphic is understanable A graph or simple chart of data sets that have different units of measure and y axis scales will only confuse the reader. Information like this is best presented as separate tables with brief concise narratives of explanation.

CHAPTER 7

Facility Condition and Capital Spending Derivatives

KPI: Record of the Top Ten Pieces of Equipment Requiring the Most CM Time and Expense

Owner	Facilities Department
Data Sources and Collection	The Facilities Department will provide the data. If there is facility maintenance management software in place, it should be able to compile most of the data needed for this report.
Reporting Frequency	Monthly

Why This KPI Is Useful

This KPI is a running record of the most troublesome plant equipment with respect to malfunctions, time, and expense for repair and comments about cause. This KPI focuses on the most persistent facility problems and does so with data. In my experience a KPI like this will become popular among employees.

Objective

Call attention to the most troublesome and serious maintenance problems affecting business. Develop a knowledge base for the most troublesome equipment to maintain. Use the knowledge base to review problems with the manufacturer or consulting engineer. Use findings to amend PM program or budget for replacement.

Managing Unfavorable Conclusions and Inferences

Work to move troublesome equipment off the list in a timely way. Do not transform the Top Ten list into a Top Fifteen or Twenty. Concentrate on the basics; a rigorous and disciplined PM program and a capital investment plan which limits the growth of deferred maintenance.

How to Calculate and/or Organize Data

See Work Sheet 7.1.

TOP TEN MOST TROUBLESOME EQUIPMENT - APRIL 2019								
Equip.	1st Month on List	House or Contract Labor?	Time Spent (hrs.)	Labor Cost	Spares or Material Cost	Total Cost	Rank Last Qtr.
AHU 5A	18-Dec	In-house	75	12,000	1,635	13,635	1
Chiller #2	18-Dec	Contract	12.5	1,875	350	2,225	1 tied
Sanitary Pit ejector Pump	19-Jan	Contract	9	1,350	750	2,100	5
Transformer 12B SWGR %	19-Jan	Contract	9	2,350	50	2,400	7
Ovhd Freight Door 3A1	19-Feb	Contract	6	1,680	300	1,980	4
AHU 3B	19-Feb	In- house	5.5	825	10	835	NR
Lighting Panel LL 260-Q	19-Feb	In- house	3.5	625	15	640	NR
Mens Rest room 1A Hall	19-Mar	In- house	4	480	380	860	2
Escalator 1A	19-Mar	Contractor	3	900	35	935	8
Ovhd Freight Door 1B1	19-Apr	Contractor	2.5	265	15	280	NR
Total			130	22,350	3,540	25,890	
What Equip. left thelist this Qtr.?	AHU 3, Elevator 5, Ovhd Door 3A2						
YTD Average # of Months before leaving list	1.3						
Last year's average	1.45						

Work Sheet 7.1 Top ten most troublesome equipment

Presentation Notes and Formats

Table which summarizes the work sheet. See Table 7.1:

TOP TEN MAINTENANCE PROBLEMS			
Equip.	On List Since	Est. Date of Repair	Spaces Affected
AHU 5A	18-Dec	30-Apr	Hall 1A
Chiller #2	18-Dec	07-May	All Exhibit Halls if promary Chiller fails
Sanitary Pit ejector Pump	19-Jan	30-Apr	Rest rooms Level 1 SW
Transformer 12B SWGR	19-Jan	10-May	Level 2 NW- Halls 1A , 1B, 1C and Mtg.rms 1 to 9
Ovhd Freight Door 3A1	19-Feb	18-Apr	3A Hall move in and out
AHU 3B	19-Feb	Apr-31	Mtg rms 15-22
Lighting Panel LL 260-Q	19-Feb	29-Apr	NW Corridors
Mens Rest room 1A Hall	19-Mar	15-May	1A Hall
Escalator 7	19-Mar	06-Apr	No.Concourse Level1 to Level 2
Ovhd Freight Door 1B1	12-Mar	31-Mar	1B Hall move in and out

Table 7.1 Top ten maintenance problems

CHAPTER 8

Human Resources Derivatives

KPI: Employee Engagement

Owner	Human Resources
Data Sources and Collection	The source of data is an employee engagement survey, administered through a human resources contractor at first, with follow-up surveys that can be handled by the Human Resources Department
Reporting Frequency	As often as necessary if human resource problems need greater clarity and a course of action.

Why This KPI Is Useful

Employee engagement measures the level of commitment employees have for their job. Employee engagement surveys are an alternative to employee satisfaction surveys. The two surveys may seem similar, but they are not. They differ in profound ways. The management consulting firm, Custominsight, describes the differences as follows:

> Employee satisfaction covers the basic concerns and needs of employees. It is a good starting point, but it usually stops short of what really matters. . . . It does not address their level of motivation, involvement, or emotional commitment. For some employees, being satisfied means collecting a paycheck while doing as little work as possible ... Employee engagement goes beyond activities, games, and events. Employee engagement drives performance.

Engaged employees look at the whole of the company and understand their purpose, where, and how they fit in. This leads to better
decision-making ... Engagement is a key differentiator.[1]

Unless senior management is solidly behind the concept of measuring
employee engagement, this KPI should be reserved for use as a problem-solving tool. Imagine a serious decline in business coupled with
growing human resource problems. There's a good possibility the two
issues are linked. This can be evidenced in data from the financial KPIs,
customer service KPIs and the "KPI Human Resource Summary," all in
Volume 1. The Employee Engagement KPI may provide the causes to this
complex problem. It is a deeper dive into the human resource health and
morale of an organization.

Objective

Learn how many employees are actively engaged in their job and how
many are not. This KPI can be a standard measuring tool for Human
Resources, a problem-solving tool or both.

When used, at some point there should be an objective to create a
work environment where the number and percentage of engaged employees increases. The expectation is that overall business performance will
improve. In 2018 the Gallup organization researched the national statistics
on engaged employees and had these findings:

- The percentage of "engaged" workers in the United States
  (those who are involved in, enthusiastic about, and committed to their work and workplace) is now 34 percent.
- Gallup also reported that 16.5 percent of workers in the
  United States were "actively disengaged."
- Those who are "actively disengaged" (have a miserable work
  experience) is now at its lowest level (13 percent). The current

---

[1] Custominsight. undated. "What is Employee Satisfaction?." https://custom-
insight.com/employee-engagement-survey/what-is-employee-satisfaction.asp
(accessed October 2019).

ratio of engaged to actively disengaged employees is now 2.6-
to -1. Gallup reports this ratio is the highest ever surveyed.

- The remaining 53 percent of workers fall in the "not engaged"
category. This does not mean their work performance is
unsatisfactory. Rather, they simply lack any strong emotional
attachment or detachment to their employer. Gallup notes
that these are the employees likely to leave for better employment opportunities.

Managing Unfavorable Conclusions and Inferences

In this circumstance, it is assumed that an employee engagement survey was conducted after an unfavorable Human Resources Summary was
exposed by KPI review. I don't believe that an unfavorable conclusion or
inference drawn by a large fraction of actively disengaged or not engaged
employees can be solved rapidly. Fixing this requires the full attention of
senior management. First, see if financial trends and productivity trends
are unfavorable. If this is the case, you indeed have a corporate morale
and culture problem. It takes a concentrated effort to cure this; structural
reorganization, targeted training programs, personnel actions, and finally
setting new goals and objectives with a schedule for continuous review
and adjustment.

How to Calculate and/or Organize Data

There will be calculations and analysis when the survey is completed.
Employee engagement survey questions should be developed specifically
to measure job performance, competency, and the sense of pride and fulfillment that comes from the organization's success. A human resources
contractor with experience in launching the survey program and inter-
preting survey scores (1 to 5) should be hired to start. Interpretation of
scores is important, a score of 4 on one question may be judged as good;
however, it may not mean the same thing on another. Engagement surveys should be statistically validated and benchmarked against other B2B
organizations. (It is doubtful whether other convention centers have conducted these surveys.) Without these things, it is difficult to know what

you are measuring and whether the results are good or bad. The business research firm, Gallup, developed an excellent employee engagement questionnaire called the "Gallup Q12 Index." It, is brief and to the point, and can be viewed through an internet search.

Presentation Notes and Formats

A statistical table showing actively engaged, engaged, and not engaged numbers and percentages of employees. This should be accompanied with a brief narrative of why and how the survey was conducted.

CHAPTER 9
Sustainability Derivatives

KPI: Water Use Per Thousand GSF Rented (KGSF)

Owner	Sustainability Manager or Facilities Department
Data Sources and Collection	Water use (per 100 gals or in hundreds of cubic feet) can be obtained from the water bills. Either the Finance Department or the Facilities Department should be responsible for keeping these records. If the water company is a city department, then the billing frequency may not be on a monthly basis and is often quarterly, semi-annually, or on irregular schedule. In these cases, you may elect to read the water meter on a regular schedule. KGSF can be obtained from the Sales Department.
Reporting Frequency	Quarterly or semi-annually

Why This KPI Is Useful

Water is a relatively inexpensive in water rich states and very expensive in states with limited resources. A water conservation program is a necessity for convention centers in states with limited water resources. In states where droughts are more frequent and severe, a more thoughtful and aggressive conservation program is also necessary to enable the center to operate without disrupting events or inconveniencing event attendees.

For some perspective, an IAVM report on Green Meetings estimated the average conference delegate uses 846 gallons of water, or roughly 262 gallons per day. Regular home use of water by the average American amounts to about 86 gallons per day.

Objective

Decrease water use as much as practical and affordable (without adversely affecting customer service) through best practices and water-saving investments.

Managing Unfavorable Conclusions and inferences

Typical investments are leak-detecting sensors and low flow sink faucets and toilets. Some convention centers have built infrastructure to capture and store storm water and use it for site irrigation.

How to Calculate and/or Organize Data

1. To best determine water use efficiency, develop water use and profile for a baseline year (a three- to five-year average) for water consumed per KGSF.
2. Follow the calculation instructions in the Work Sheet 9.1.

BASELINE WATER USE EFFICIENCT			
WATER USE	CCF	KGSF Rented	CCF per KGSF Rented
1st Qtr.	48,000	5,838	8.2
2nd Qtr.	56,950	6,436	8.8
TOTAL	104,950	12,274	8.6
CURRENT WATER USE EFFICIENCY			
WATER USE	CCF	KGSF Rented	CCF per KGSF Rented
1st Qtr.	34,050	5,984	5.7
2nd Qtr.	49,500	6,533	7.6
TOTAL	83,550	12,517	6.7
SAVINGS DUE TO CHANGE IN EFFICIENCY (3.4%)			
CCF Saved	Price/CCF	$ Avoided/ Saved	
23,478	$2.15	$505	
Gals. Saved			
17,514,435			

Work Sheet 9.1 Water use efficiency

Calculation Instructions:

1. To calculate the water saved in hundreds of cubic feet (CCF), multiply the KGSF for the current year by the baseline year CCF per KGSF Rented and then subtract the product by current year's total water use.
2. To calculate gallons of water saved, multiply CCF Saved by 748 (there are 748 gallons of water per CCF).

Presentation Format

Table, bar graph, or both comparing current YTD, previous YTD and business plan.

KPI: Report on Sustainability Initiatives

Owner	Sustainability Manager
Data Sources and Collection	The Sustainability Manager should compose an interesting narrative of each initiative and keep a record of measureable results.
Reporting Frequency	Semi-annually

Why This KPI Is Useful

A series of progress reports on sustainability initiatives will be interesting and well read. Sustainability initiatives are good topics to include as content for enhancing your center's social media presence.

Convention centers are excellent demonstration sites or laboratories for promoting viable sustainability. They are highly visible to businesspeople, media, professionals, and interested public who may be attending or exhibiting at events. Below are examples of sustainability initiatives worth tracking and reporting:

- On-site generation of electricity though solar or wind power.
- On-site storage of electricity produced with renewable energy.

- Green roofs and other natural settings on the property. Convention centers have two outstanding demonstrations of green roofs at the Vancouver Convention and Exhibition Centre and the Javits Center.
- Reduction of plastic throw away bottles.
- Compostable food packaging.
- On-site food production (herb gardens, vegetables, mini orchards).
- On-site display of electric cars (ideally through an automobile company sponsorship).
- Recharging stations in parking areas for electric vehicles.

Objective

Engage in as many viable sustainability initiatives as practical. Initiatives are viable in the sense that the initiatives are new and emerging technologies, methods, and practices that may serve as visible working examples and speed commercialization. At some point, if the initiative or project is commercial viability it may qualify for further investment.

Managing Unfavorable Conclusions and Inferences

This KPI should be active with new data and information all the time. Presently the list of new initiatives is plentiful. If inactive, have a serious discussion with the center's Sustainability Manager.

How to Calculate and/or Organize Data

No calculations are necessary other than converting units of measure into pounds or tons of CO_2.

Presentation Notes and Formats

The presentation format should be a brief narrative of progress, possibly with photos and preliminary results of savings, carbon footprint reduction, return on investment, and so on.

CHAPTER 10

Presenting and Displaying KPIs

Throughout Volumes 1 and 2, you have seen examples of presentations of how to present KPI data using graphs, charts and tables. Know that your efforts may come to this; all the hard work and time spent developing a KPI program may be to no effect if not communicated well. The primary recipient for the facts, trends, and insights a KPI program imparts are the convention center employees. This is not just managers and sales team but also the customer service reps, security guards, rank-and-file tradesmen, cleaners, waitresses, cashiers, indeed all those who do the work. They have to see the program come to life and grow. Communicating results properly will induce employees to think about the meaning of the information presented and their role and contribution. It may even motivate and inspire.

Best practices regarding "how to" present data in an orderly and effective form all seem to originate with a statistician and prolific writer and lecturer on the subject, Edward R. Tufte. His insight on simplicity and clarity is instructive. Tufte believes that the best methods for analyzing and communicating statistical information are usually the simplest and at the same time the most powerful. The most effective way to describe, explore, and summarize a set of numbers even a very large set is to look at pictures of those numbers. Tufte explains this: "the consequences of poorly presented graphics are mundane—wasted time and an audience bored into cynicism or slumber." His basic advice on graphics is to:

- show the data;
- induce viewers to think about the substance rather than about design concepts and techniques, the technology of graphic production, or something else;

- not overdo and distort what the data have to say;
- not overload by presenting too many numbers in a small space;
- make large data sets understandable;
- make certain any graphics are closely related to statistical tables and written or verbal descriptions of the data

For convention centers, there are few if any reasons to present KPIs using sophisticated graphics beyond tables, graphs, charts, and simple condensed narratives or combinations of all. KPI messaging can be confused or lost if the presentation overreaches and fails to connect with the reader.

Tables

Tables are effective when displaying single categories of information, which were measured at different time intervals. An example would be to measure the number of events held quarterly, profits earned per month, or electricity consumed per quarter. Tables are the preferred means of presentation when there are small data sets. Tufte states that tables usually outperform graphics in reporting on data sets of 20 numbers or less. And yes, there is a discipline for table design. Rather than going into all the techniques, the best advice is to think "simplicity." See the examples tables in Table 10.1—one table designed properly and the other poorly:

Table 10.1 Comparison of a well designed vs. poorly designed table

WELL DESIGNED TABLE		POORLY DESIGNED TABLE		
Economic Sector	**Year-to-Date %**			
Consumer Goods	15	Health/Life Science		8.70%
SMERF	12	Fashion		11.59%
Fashion	12	IT	7.97%	
Arts, Sports and Leisure	9	Consumer Goods		14.49%
Health/Life Science	9	Arts, Sports and Leisure		9.42%
Hobbyists/Collect-ibles	9	Manufacturing/Ind./Const.		6.52%
Finance/Investing	9	Food		5.07%
Tech	8	Hobbyists/Collectibles	8.70%	
Manufacturing/Ind./ Const.	7	SMERF		11.59%
Food	5	Finance/Investing		8.70%
Other	5	Professional Services		2.17%
Professional Services	2	Other		5.07%

Source: Captal City Convention
Center- Annual Report- 2019

The table on the above right is considered poor design because of the following reasons:

1. It has no title and the columns are not labeled.
2. There are too many gridlines. Overbusy gridlines distract.
3. The percent notation is unnecessary and carrying percent to two decimal spaces is superfluous.
4. The order of rows is random. It would be easier to follow if the rows were arranged as the number order is arranged; the highest percentage is first and then listed in descending order as shown in the well-designed table.

5. Placement of data and text within cells is not uniform. It is irregular and distracting to the reader

6. There is no source for the data listed.

The well-designed table is better because it displays the same information in a simpler and easy-to-follow format.

Graphs and Charts

Graphs and charts should be used when a visual image simplifies information and shows trends. They are also useful when making comparisons to baseline and previous year statistics, benchmarks, and the business plan or forecast. Good graph and chart design require consideration of some key elements. Figure 10.1 maps the elements:

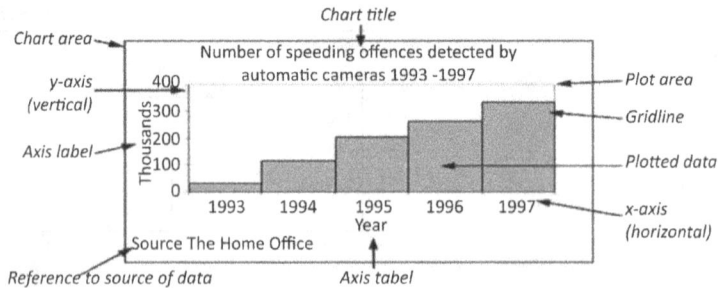

Figure 10.1 Components of a graph

Source: Presenting Numerical Data, University of Leicester, Undated.

The list below explains the elements:

1. *Chart area*: This area sets boundaries for all graph or chart elements. It is the first step and necessary so all elements are considered as one, separate from the surrounding text. Chart area can be invisible or drawn in as a frame.

2. *Plot area*: Plot area is the graph section with the data bordered by the *x* and *y* axes.

3. *Gridlines*: Gridlines are vertical or horizontal lines drawn in the plot area. They should be used sparingly and only when they aid in reading the graph. Otherwise they only detract. Gridlines are usually drawn at regular, logical intervals along the *y*-axis.

4. *Titles*: The title identifies and describes the data being reviewed. It should be placed above the top of the plot area, horizontally centered to be read from left to right. A well-composed title will reduce the need for extra explanatory labeling, which can be a distraction.

5. *Labels*: Use labels to avoid distortions and ambiguities that may come from the graph itself. Compose in a clear and detailed manner and place in the graphic. Avoid uncommon abbreviations and avoid too many labels. Labels can be used for a brief explanation of the data or to point out noteworthy events.

6. *Color and shading*: In bar charts, pie charts, and to a lesser extent line graphs color and shading are often used to distinguish between different categories and timelines. Experts advise that choices among colors be gradations of the same color going from dark tones to light or vice versa. Tufte advises that ". . . the mind's eye does not readily give a visual ordering to colors, except possibly for red to reflect higher levels than other colors." Tufte has a strong preference to gray and shades of gray. He explains, "The success of gray compared to the visually more spectacular color gives us a lead on how multi-functioning graphical elements can communicate complex information without turning into puzzles. The shades of gray provide an easily comprehended order to the data measures. This is the key." I believe Tufte's gray coloration works well until there are more than three data sets. It becomes difficult to identify separate pieces or displays of data. At that point (given the limitations of your graphic software), you simply run out of shades of gray. Multiple colors is a reasonable alternative in this circumstance.

Bar Graphs

For visualizing data, the type graph used most frequently is a bar graph. They are best choice when displaying and comparing data amounts and productivity measures over time (quarterly, semi-annually, or annually) and in relation to baseline data, previous years, benchmarks, or the business plan. Bar graphs are versatile and can be drawn in a variety of ways: drawn vertically where the taller bar is largest in the category, drawn horizontally when there is plot area space limitations or, drawn grouped when showing information about different subgroups of the main category (see Figure 10.2).

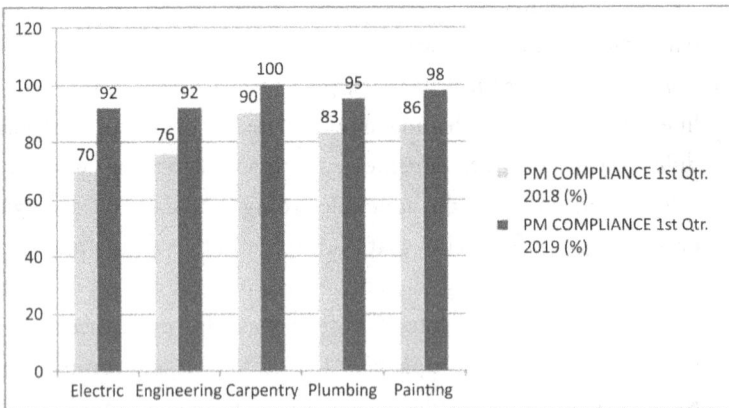

Figure 10.2 Example of a bar graph

I favor bar graphs when presenting KPIs because they:

- best display KPI changes over time when the time intervals are quarterly, semiannually, or annually;
- summarize a large data set in visual form thus enabling the reader to estimate key values at a glance;
- display relative numbers or proportions of multiple categories;
- permit a visual check of the accuracy and reasonableness of calculations; and
- are easily understood due to widespread use in business and the media.

Line Graphs

A line graph is most often used to track changes over short and long periods of time, particularly when the time durations during periods are short and in sequence, by month for example. Line graphs are useful in that they show data variables and trends clearly and can help to make predictions about the results of data not yet recorded. They can also be used to display several dependent variables against one independent variable. When comparing data sets, line graphs are only useful if the axes follow the same scales. Experts recommend no more than four lines on a single graph; any more than that and it becomes difficult for the reader to interpret (Figure 10.3).

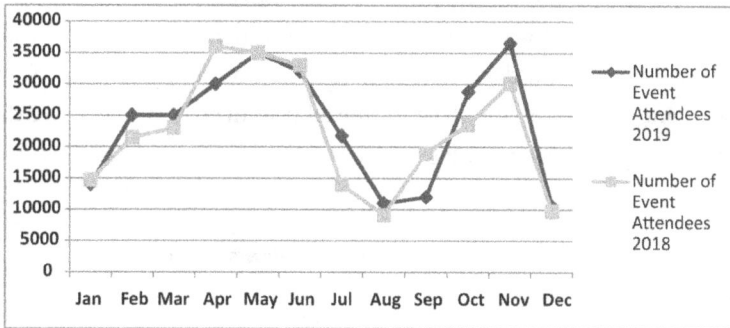

Figure 10.3 Example of a line graph

Line graphs are appropriate for presenting KPIs because they

- best display KPI changes over time when the time intervals are monthly;
- are easy to read; they present data trends in the most basic form, a horizontal line sloping up or down; and
- make it easy to see relationships between independent sets of data, say Number of Events or current Occupancy Rate compared to years past.

Pie Charts

Pie charts are a graphical way showing information such as percentages of earned revenue by profit center. They are not favored by graphic experts and should only be used when the number of categories is small, say about 5. However, some viewers like them because they are simple and familiar. My opinion is that the disadvantages of using a pie chart outweigh the advantages. Pie charts do not reveal exact values nor show changes in data over time nor show causes, effects, trends, or patterns.

There are two alternative methods of displaying data which fit a KPI presentation; simple statistical tables and ring charts.

A table is always preferred to a pie chart. With a pie chart, the viewer has to compare quantities located in "spatial disarray." One has to work to match the legend with the correct "pie slice," the multi-coloring of the pie is confusing, and the entire graphic takes up too much space. Why would one substitute a pie chart for the table to display this data? See the contrast of presentations in Figure 10.4:

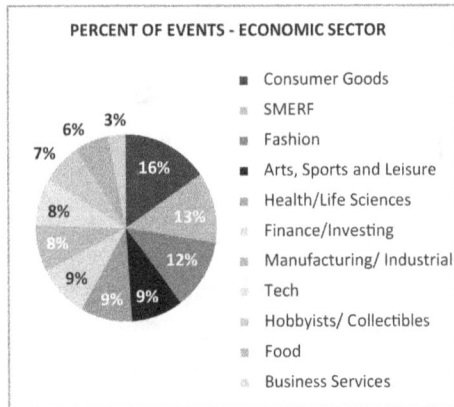

PERCENT OF EVENTS - ECONOMIC SECTOR	%
Consumer Goods	15
SMERF	12
Fashion	12
Arts, Sports and Leisure	9
Health/Life Sciences	9
Finance/Investing	9
Manufacturing/ Industrial	8
Tech	8
Hobbyists/ Collectibles	7
Food	6
Business Services	3

Figure 10.4 Comparison of a table to a pie chart

If the KPI program gets more attention with graphics, compare the pie chart to a segmented ring chart. See the comparison in Figure 10.5:

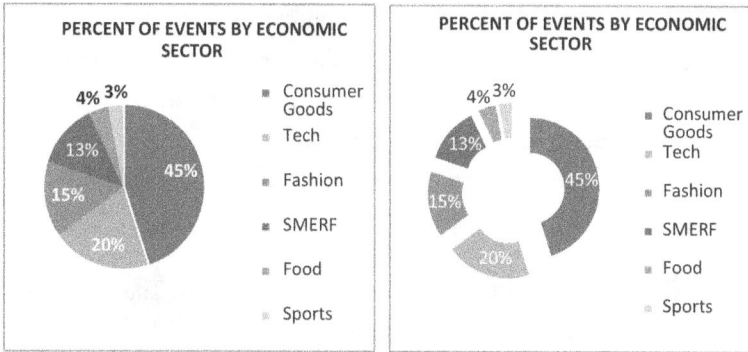

Figure 10.5 Comparison of a pie chart to segmented ring chart

Typography and Fonts

Typography is the visual component of written text. It refers to the rules governing the composition of type into legible text. Fonts are combination of typeface and other qualities, such as size, shape, letter dimensions, and spacing. Choosing the correct typography and font is no small matter. In implementing a KPI program, the choice of font to improve readability and appearance can affect the overall presentation. A piece was posted on the endgadget.com website that covers this subject well. Their piece is paraphrased below:

1. It's the principal means of communicating business information to employees, board members, and stakeholders.
2. If well-crafted and organized in a manner where the content flows logically it will attract readers and hold their attention. Correct fonts add value to the graphic and adjoining text and helps readers better perceive the information.
3. Correct fonts help form a certain impression. In the case of a KPI presentation, that impression should be one of clear communication of information and data, factual and unambiguous.
4. Fonts establish an information hierarchy where the content flows in an organized progression. This can be done with font sizing, capitalizing, using bold text, or highlighting.

5. Proper typography and font selection create harmony in presentations. Using the same font for similar content provides continuity. Alignment of fonts in correct proportion organizes a presentation and provides an uncluttered appearance.

6. All of the above reflects thoughtfulness, competence, and professionalism.

So what is the appropriate font for KPI presentations? There are several favored by the graphic design community: Verdana, Helvetia, Tahoma, Georgia, and Calibri. Tufte's preference is Gill Sans, which is not available on MS Outlook's tool bar and menu.

For practical reasons, I recommend Calibri as the font for KPI presentations. Calibri 10 is the default font for MS Excel where most of a KPI's work sheets and probably presentations will originate. MS went to this because of the growth and proliferation of "digital consumption," meaning their business forecasts showed that most readers would eventually view numeric reports and tables on mobile devices like iPhones and tablets. Calibri was the best choice for viewing on those devices and it read well when viewed on laptops and print also. I rely on the professional experience and wisdom of Microsoft.

"Chart Junk"

Tufte again originated and first described chart junk. He spends a good deal of his writing and lectures preaching against it. The simplest definition of chart junk I could find comes from the eagereyes.org website: "Any ink on your chart that does not convey data is considered junk."[1]

Some examples of chart junk include:

- Clip art
- Excessive coloration
- Backgrounds and photos
- 3D graphics
- Textures, unnecessary shading, and gradients

---

[1] Kosara, R., March 17, 2013. "A Better Definition of Chart Junk." https://eagereyes.org/blog/2013/definition-chart-junk (accessed September 2019).

- Too many gridlines
- Unnecessary labeling
- Form changes, for example, tilting a bar graph.

Dashboards

Everybody loves dashboards. In my time as a consultant, I have seen them prominently posted in large format on bulletin boards for all employees to see, in annual reports which the public may see, as excerpts to enhance a magazine story, and so on. Dashboards can be creatively designed to fit a particular audiences interest. Designed properly, dashboards are powerful and effective. Michael Alexander of Microsoft authored, "Excel Dashboards and Reports for Dummies." In it he describes dashboards as:"… a visual interface that provides at-a-glance views into key measures relevant to a particular objective or business process."[2]

A dashboard's key attributes are further described as:

- Graphic in nature to focusing on "key trends, comparisons and exceptions."
- Displaying only relevant data to the dashboards subject matter.
- Containing "inherently predefined conclusions," relieving viewers from further analysis.

I personally wouldn't get too carried away with the above description, especially when KPIs have multiple parts each requiring a clear understanding before reading on. There are cases where a dashboard graphic needs and is complemented by adjoining narrative, best composed in short concise sentences. Do not rely on a bullet list format, which are overly generic and often fail to explain in full how a particular KPI works.

---

[2] Alexander, M. 2016. *Excel Dashboards and Reports for Dummies*, Chichester, UK, John Wiley & Sons, p.10.

In the graphic shown in Figure 10.6, I show an example of a dashboard where there are brief narratives emphasizing how the achievements are depicted with KPI data and results. The dashboard was done on Excel. It is relatively simple and understandable. Dashboards can often overreach with excessive color, overloads of data, and lack of a sequencing of relevant information. They can easily become garish and confusing.

Take the time to do an internet search of KPI dashboard images.

This figure along with the accompanying text should all be on the same page.

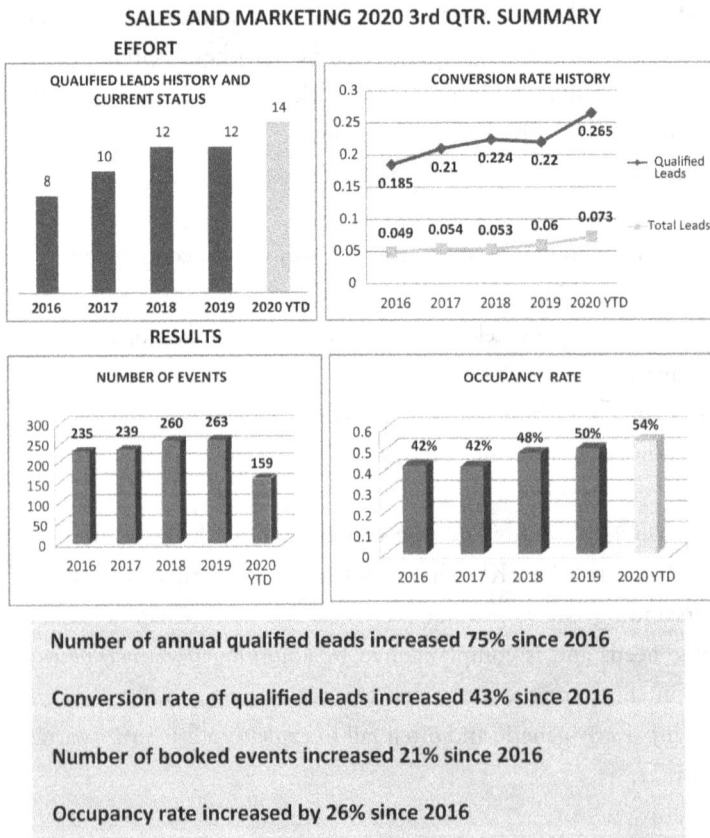

Figure 10.6 Sales and marketing 2020 3rd Qtr. Summary (dashboard)

CHAPTER 11

Framework and Context and Steps for Implementing a KPI Program

A beginner's mistake is to fill KPI programs with as many KPIs as possible to cover any situation or contingency no matter the relevance or importance. To launch an effective business analytics/KPI program, an organization must decide on what really matters and which methods of data collection and analysis provide the best problem-solving answers. Convention centers already collect a great deal of data, but it has to be organized and weighed before deciding which data are to be integrated into a KPI program.

Knowing the demands on management time, how can KPIs be crafted into logical and workable segments? KPIs need a framework or context that is familiar to employees already. Mixing new techniques, KPI buzzwords, and workflow diagrams from other industries confuses the process further. Centers need their own KPI framework and strategic and operational elements. My recommendation is to either organize data and KPIs into the departments and divisions responsible for each KPI, or use the strategy elements introduced in Chapter 1 as a model framework. See Work Sheet 11.1:

CONVENTION CENTER KPI FRAMEWORK (Examples)	
LEADERSHIP AND GOVERNANCE	**ECONOMIC IMPACT**
Monthly Financial Report	Economic Impact
Monthly Profit per GSF	Market Share of Certain Event Types
Occupancy Rate	Lost Business Report
Profit / GSF - Each Event Type	Net Promoter Score
OPERATIONAL AND BUSINESS COMPETENCY	**OVERALL FINANCIAL HEALTH**
Conversion Rates per Qualified Lead	Monthly Profit per GSF
Profit per GSF for Each Event Type	Capital Reserve Status
Electric Service Profit per NSF	Operating Expense Percentages by Category
Customer Complaints	

Work Sheet 11.1 Convention center KPI framework (examples)

Implementation Steps

Step 1: Commit to Constant Improvement and Growth

Senior management and the Board of Directors have to be fully committed to the program and find competent managers motivated to the cause. The value of good middle managers cannot be overemphasized. Productivity excellence and quality of managers are inextricably tied together.

Step 2: Define the Program's Principal Objectives

Start with the essentials of a center's business strategy and build from there. For a convention center the elements of strategy are:

- *Leadership and Governance:* Having the right management structure and governance in place; competent, well informed, decisive, and committed to constant improvement.
- *Economic Impact:* Achieving high occupancy and attracting enough out-of-town visitors to materially improve profits for hotels, restaurants, and entertainment and cultural attractions.
- *Operational and Business Competency:* Maintaining high standards of customer service with respect to building appearance, functionality and efficiency, and event services.

- *Overall Financial Health:* Contributing enough earned revenue to reduce dependence on subsidies, maintain positive cash flow, and establish a capital reserve.

Step 3: Include Business Activity Statistics and Guard from Overreliance on Financial Reports

Financial KPIs alone are not enough. They do not capture the value-creating activities. The statistics convention centers use to track and communicate performance always include financial reports and economic impact summaries. However, they have only a faint connection to the objectives of improving revenue and service, customer satisfaction, or gaining market share.

Step 4: Develop KPIs that Best Achieve Objectives

Is there confidence that improvement through selected KPIs will achieve objectives? Spend time talking this through. Hear what your line managers and house and event floor supervision have to say.

Step 5: Take the Next Step—Implement the KPI Program

Follow this sequence:

1. It would be a mistake to assign this project as extra work to an existing manager. It's too important and to stop and restart when convenient; you will lose momentum. Start by assigning or hiring a project manager to manage the KPI launch and train staff. This individual must understand the KPI process, know how the convention center works, demonstrate proficiency in MS Excel and MS Power BI or equivalent, be able to identify information sources, and understand techniques and logic of graphic presentations.

2. My personal view is that adequate graphic presentations and dashboards can be created using MS Excel and sometimes MS Power Point. This is especially true for a convention center just launching a KPI program. If a greater level of sophistication is needed, then I would consider MS Power BI. Power BI is a business intelligence

platform that provides nontechnical business users with tools for aggregating, analyzing, visualizing, and sharing data. I recommend reviewing the comparisons between Excel and Power BI. A good source is to visit this website, https://educba.com/power-bi-vs-excel/

3. During development the project manager will work closely with line managers who will "own" KPIs related to their job.

4. Before eliminating KPIs from your program and proceeding with data sources and collection and development of work sheets, consider the advantages of linking KPIs to selected KPI worksheets. See the "Linking KPIs—Automatically Updating Data from one Excel Sheet to Another" section that follows.

5. Start with the fundamental KPIs and major revenue sources and "soft launch." Eventually work up to include other KPIs and derivatives such as productivity metrics.

6. Control the format for KPI presentations. A good idea would be to create a KPI Book, organized by departments or the Framework elements described above or both. Publish digitally and in print. When employees start asking "what time today is the KPI Book coming out?" you'll know the KPI program has been accepted.

7. Control the schedule of the KPI Book, say every six weeks and control the distribution of the KPI Book and/or excerpts.

Step 6: Assess KPI Validity after a Few Months and Add, Delete, or Revise as Necessary

Test the KPIs for their usefulness in achieving objectives. Look for these two important qualities:

- *Persistence*, where outcomes of an action at one time repeat consistently, and
- *Predictability*, proving the reliability of causal relationships between the action and outcome.

Linking KPIs—Automatically Updating Data from One Excel Sheet to Another

Worksheets can be updated with data from another Excel Workbook sheet automatically. A link is a dynamic formula that pulls data from a cell of one worksheet and updates that data to another worksheet. These linking worksheets can be in the same workbook or in another workbook. One worksheet is called the **source worksheet**, from where this link pulls the data, and the other worksheet is called the **destination worksheet** that contains that link formula and where data is updated automatically. For those unfamiliar with the Excel linking features, an excellent website is available with easy – to – follow explanations and instructions, https://help.smartsheet.com/articles/861579-cell-linking.

Consider the advantages of linking KPI work sheets and tables using Excel:

- Less administrative work when assembling KPI presentations or the KPI Book.
- More timely KPI reports. If an End of Event Report (see Work Sheets 11.2 through 11.2f) completed within a few days after each event closes, this is as close to"real time"reporting you can get for many importatnt KPIs.
- A knowledge base of important metrics and indicators for each event type and economic sector. Data based decision making is superior decision making.
- Use this as a model to obtain other KPIs with less admin work and more timely results. For example, if you use "KPI: Economic Impact of Convention Center Events" (from Volume 1) and complete Work Sheet 1.4A Monthly Economic Impact of Events (short version) in Excel, then you can obtain a very current record of economic impact and present it in table and/or graphic form for KPI presentations and the KPI Book.
- As the program matures, the data base will become more and more accurate. Business forcasting will in turn become more accurate. The data base for each event type and economic sector can be transformed into an accurate profile of exhibitor spending and customer service issues. This can be combined at some point with economic impact.

All the above can best be accomplished by doing a comprehensive "end of event" report. If linked proerly this report will automatically update many other KPIs.Review Work Sheet 11.2 End of Event Report below:

END OF EVENT REPORT					
Event Name		Move In Dates		GSC	
Event Type		Event Dates		NSF	
Event Sector		Move Out Dates		GSF Rented	

Work Sheet 11.2 End of event report

PART ONE - EVENT PROFIT/LOSS STATEMENT										
	ACTUAL								PLAN	
Category	Rev. or Comm.	# of Bill. Items	Labor Hrs.	Labor Costs	Material Cost Est.	Total Costs	Profit	Variance from Plan	Profit or Comm.	Profit or Comm./ GSF Rented
Rent										
Electric										
Plumbing										
Parking										
F & B										
Comm.										
Cleaning										
A/V										
Set- Up										
Adv.										
Rigging										
Security										
Medical										
Other										
Sub- totals										
Overall Event										
EVENT ORGANIZER'S COMMENTS										

Work Sheet 11.2a End of event report (cont'd)

	PART TWO - EARNED REVENUE AND OVERALL EVENT PRODUCTIVITY METRICS							
Category	Profit or Comm. / GSF	Profit or Comm. / NSF	Labor Hrs./ Bill. Item	Labor Costs/ GSF	Order Fulfil-ment %	Variance from Type Average	Variance from Sector Average	Remarks
Rent	NA	NA	NA					
Electric								
Plumbing								
Parking		NA						
F & B		NA						
Comms.								
Cleaning								
A/V								
Set- Up		NA						
Adv.								
Rigging								
Security								
Other								
Sub-totals								
Overall Event								

Work Sheet 11.2b - End of event report (cont'd)

PART THREE - EVENT SERVICE COMPLAINTS AND NET PROMOTER SCORE (NPS)									
Events	F & B	Utility Service	Parking	Comms.	Cleaning	Other	Sub - Total	% of Total	Remarks
Quality of Work									
Quality of Food		NA	NA	NA	NA	NA			
Delays / Slow Service									
Appearance									
Rudeness									
Price									
Wi Fi Speed									
WiFi Reliability									
Other									
Total									
NPS Record				Remarks					
2nd to the last Score									
Last Score									
Current Score									

Work Sheet 11.2c End of event report (cont'd)

PART FOUR - FACILITY COMPLAINTS			
Facility	# of Complaints	% of Total	Remarks
HVAC Cold			
HVAC Hot			
Way finding			
Restroom Cleanling			
Elevators			
Escalators			
Safety			
Security			
Snow and Ice Removal			
Business Center			
Coat and Luggage Check			
Transportation Pick up/ Drop- off			
Taxi, Uber Lyft Service			
Other			

Work Sheet 11.2d End of event report (cont'd)

PART FIVE - RECORD OF SECURITY INCIDENTS					
Credible Threats	**# of Incidents**	**Remarks**	**Security Incidents**	**#**	**Remarks**
Terrorism			Theft		
Violence			Vandalism		
Criminality			Disord. Conduct		
Event Disruption			Fraud		
Other			Assault		
			Other		
Total			Total		

Work Sheet 11.2e End of event report (cont'd)

PART SIX - RECORD OF SAFETY INCIDENTS					
Injuries	**#**	**Remarks**	**Illnesses**	**#**	**Remarks**
Slip and Fall			Heat Related		
Fall From Heights			Food Related		
Hit by Object from Above			Seizure		
Hit by Moving Veh.			Infect Disease		
Elec. Shocked			Other		
Other					
Near Misses	**#**	**Remarks**			
Driving Too Fast					
Driving Recklessly					
Improper Use of Ladder					
Improper Use of Power Tools					
Unsafe Electrical install					
No Fall Protection					
No Safe Zone Below When Working Aloft					
Other					

Work Sheet 11.2f - End of event report (cont'd)

CHAPTER 12

Last Word

In tourist-based economies, convention centers are a major cog in the wheel of commerce. Las Vegas, Orlando, and New Orleans are the most prominent. However, on a national scale we are a small but visible species of business. Many depend on us; professional and trade associations, tradeshow organizers, corporations, business startups, and the general public. They count on and appreciate our scale, our physical plant and service capacity, and the roles we play in the production of events and mass meetings. We are the grand market and meeting place and we fulfill the business and professional goals of sales, marketing, branding, product rollouts, continuing education, and face-to-face communications and networking. Convention centers share the same mission. We also share the same vulnerabilities, such as:

- *An oversupply of convention center space.* In the U. S. this is evidenced by occupancy rates that probably average only 50 percent among top tier cities and less for smaller cities. The "market price" for convention center space rent lies at the point between the available supply and demand. Clearly the over-supply of exhibit space has influenced and driven down rent. Among event organizers space rent is considered inexpensive in the United States when compared to Europe where the market price for space rent is three or more times greater.

- *A limited business model:*
  A convention center's building configuration and space is mostly programmed for hosting large exhibitions; conventions with exhibits, tradeshows and consumer shows. This design process has been largely influenced by two factors:

1. Creation of an environment where events can profit by selling exhibit space and organizing the show floor for easy way-finding. This means modular single story space, with high ceilings, similar contiguous space for event expansion and generous distances between columns.

2. Site and building features that reduce the cost of freight shipping and handling; accessible roadways that accommodate large trucks, ample loading dock space, multiple freight doors, and space for empty crate storage.

By contrast, indoor arenas are able to be versatile and adaptive in ways that most convention centers cannot. Their oval shaped bowl configuration with fixed tired seating, high visibility video screens, and level event floor permit a wide diversity of events; major league, collegiate and interscholastic sports, concerts, large religious and political gatherings, e-sports competitions, small trade and consumer shows and more.

Business model limitations are further explained as many convention centers have been influenced by this oft-repeated legacy that "convention centers are not designed to make a profit". Although this idea is fading, center management understands that long ago many centers acceded major portions of the event service business to others like GSCs and event organizers. While most centers hold exclusive rights for food and beverage and communications services, management is reluctant to engage in claiming exclusivity or competing for other services. They know there will be legal challenges and unfavorable publicity. Event organizers will aggressively defend choosing their own service contractors and benefitting from the commissions they receive. As of now, centers are left with few earned revenue opportunities.

How are convention centers different?

Clearly, cities where convention centers are located with their local culture, economic base, transportation access, hotel inventory, and even weather have a profound effect on marketability. From a customer service standpoint, there are some sensitive touch points that differentiate; union labor work rules and hourly rates, food and beverage quality and prices, safety and security, ambiance and comfort, and interactions with center employees. Some convention centers succeed at this better than others.

From a financial standpoint, differences are evident when reviewing audited financial statements. They show most convention centers relying on subsidies to pay expenses and fund capital improvements. I have read many of these statements and I am always surprised to see the amount of subsidies required to just conduct routine business. The difference in financial statements from the few convention centers that operate at positive cash flow is mostly due to earned revenue.

I am an advocate for KPI programs and also a practitioner. In my time at the Javits Center we relied heavily on KPIs. Javits Center's KPI program was improvised and did not have the structured quality as the process is now. Our program was closely held among key managers and field supervisors with no KPI displays or dashboards. We concentrated on sales, the performance of retained events, productivity metrics related to event services and energy management. The Javits Center was and is still profitable and has built and maintained a substantial capital reserve.

If your center is not actively engaged in tracking KPIs, consider starting. If you only track high level strategic KPIs, you need to dive deeper and track the tactical metrics which affect earned revenues, expenses and customer service. This means involving all employees which may be a big change but a positive culture shift. To review, here's what a well-crafted KPI program can achieve:

- *Order and Simplicity:* Once launched, debugged and trial runs completed, the program will reduce manual and improvised reports as well as mistakes and errors. The KPI process in full has the attributes of standardization and orderly coordination.
- *Improvements in Earned Revenue and Expense Control:* Tracking productivity metrics and reviewing trends exposes ineffective management practices and reveals opportunities for improvement. Once underway a KPI program will likely improve financial results by 10 percent and establish some-

thing to build on. If you are fortunate, some of the profits can be used to start a capital reserve. When the reserve accumulates you will have the freedom to invest your capital and keep up with tired building elements such as, worn carpet and outdated interior décor, or keep pace with new communications infrastructure or energy efficient equipment.

- *Strengthen Organizational Responsiveness:* With KPIs you will not have to rely on intuition or "gut feeling". When deciding on a course of action, there is no more effective business tool than the facts, data, and insight obtained through a KPI program. Once supervisory employees are engaged in the KPI process, they can be empowered to make the correct field decisions when setting up an event or dealing with exhibitors and attendees. This new confidence and agility are competencies that lead to customer service excellence.

"It is the mark of a truly intelligent person to be moved by statistics." This is a quote from George Bernard Shaw, noted playwright and author. He wrote *Man and Superman, Pygmalion*, et al.[1]

---

[1] Shaw, G.B. undated. https://allauthor.com/quotes/31215/ (accessed December 2019).

Addendum

The COVID - 19 Pandemic

As this book is being edited and published, the COVID – 19 Pandemic has made its mark, and radically changed business and daily life. Convention centers around the nation have been converted into field hospitals, medical testing sites, and supply depots. Events cancelled and for a short time in March organizers nervously jockeyed for alternative event dates in the late summer or fall. Meanwhile hotel occupancy dropped precipitously. The research firm and consultancy, HVS, has projected that if the current level of RevPARs firm continues throughout April, RevPARs will reach $15.61 from a pre-crisis level of $116.97, an 86.7% decline from the prior year. Their research covers 24 major markets throughout the country. In Orlando it has been reported that hote;l taxes have evaporated from $26 million in 2019 to less than $800,000. The effect of the COVID-19 pandemic on hotel tax revenue presents serious challenges to convention centers that are dependent on this revenue stream. Hotel taxes in most jurisdictions pay the debt service on the bonds which funded convention center construction. Moreover the taxes are also a revenue source that covers operating deficits for many convention centers.

The Javits Center experienced something like this during the 9/11 attack. We evacuated and mobilized as a site for medical treatment of the injured and base for rescue teams, police, and the National Guard. Events cancelled and we were out of business for three months. The Javits Center business recovery after 9/11 was V – shaped. The business recovery after the Great Recession of 2008 and 2009 was rapid but more U-shaped. By the 2nd quarter of 2010, the event industry was back, tracking consistently with a growing GDP.

Similarities between then and now with the pandemic disruption of the global economy end there however. The profundity of the virus eludes explanation making recovery estimates and timing uncertain. A second wave of the virus seems certain without a vaccine. An article in the April 18 – 19 issue of *The Wall Street Journal* described the next six months for mass gatherings like this, "… the darkest shadow hanging over the future of sports, concerts and every type of mass gathering that was commonplace before. . . .Second waves are inevitable in pandemics when you don't have a vaccine."[1]

It's late June now and there is faint evidence that convention centers will keep soldiering on; CES appears determined to hold their massive tradeshow this January in Las Vegas with plenty of safeguards; Orange County Convention Center will re-open in July with a large sporting event, and Messe Munich in Germany is prepared to re-open their tradefair campus for events in September.

From The Plague by Albert Camus; "And indeed it could be said that once the faintest stirring of hope became possible, the dominion of plaugue was ended."[2]

---

[1] Radnofsky, L. and Cohen, B., April 18-19, 2020, "Sports Eye Second Wave as New Risk", *The Wall Street Journal*, p. A3.

[2] Camus, Albert, 1947. www.goodreads.com/quotes/147920

References

Chapter 1

McMillin, D. *undated.* "Real Reason Convention Center Attendees are not Booking in the Block" https://pcma.org/room-block-study-why-convention-attendees-dont-book-room-block/ (accessed February 2019).

Hazinski, T.A. February 5, 2010. "How Convention Centers Influence Hotel Markets." https://hvs.com/article/4405-how-convention-centers-influence-hotel-markets (accessed November 2019).

Ricca, S. August 22, 2018. "A Look at Convention Center Impact on Hotel Submarkets." http://hotelnewsnow.com/Articles/289070/A-look-at-convention-center-impact-on-hotel-submarkets

Las Vegas Convention and Visitors Authority. undated. "Tourism Industry and Convention Sector, June 2019 – Revised."

Hanna, R. 2018. "What's So Hot About the Hotel Occupancy Tax." *Abilene Reporter News*, April 12, 2018, https://reporternews.com/story/news/2018/04/12/whats-so-hot-hotel-occupancy-tax/488037002/ (accessed October 2019).

Conroy, B. January/February 2020, "The Washington State Convention Center's New Addition Will Create Big Bucks." *seattlebusinessmag.com*, (accessed January 2020).

HVS, December 18, 2018. "Lancaster County Convention Center." *Impact Study*, December 18, 2018, http://lccca.com/wp-content/uploads/2018/12/HVS-LCCC-Report-Final-12-18-2018.pdf (accessed October 2019).

IMPLAN. May, 2019. "Employment FAQ." https://implanhelp.zendesk.com/hc/en-us/articles/115009510967-Employment-FAQ (accessed December 2019).

Van Deventer, P., and Harper, R. 2017. "Defining Conventions as Urban Innovation and Economic Accelerators." https://meetingsmeanbusiness.com/sites/default/files/SkiftMMB-Defining-Conventions-As-Urban-Innovation-And-Economic-Accellerators-Report.pdf (accessed August 2019).

Chapter 2

Soffer, Ari, July 5, 2019, "Marketing Effectiveness - What it Means and 4 Ways to Measure it." https://www.leadspace.com/marketing-effectiveness/ (accessed May, 2020).

Bernard, M. 2012. *Key Performance Indicators*, Edinburgh Gate, Harlow UK, Pearson Education Limited.

Hausman, A. February 26, 2019. "5 Reasons B2B Companies Should Use Social Media Marketing." https://marketinginsidergroup.com/social-media/b2b-social-media-marketing/ (accessed December 2019).

Schrage, M. November 21, 2011. "A Better Way to Handle Publically Tweeted Complaints." https://hbr.org/2011/11/a-better-way-to-handle-publicl.html (accessed November 2019).

Bredava, A. May 19, 2019. "5 Tools to Track Brand Mentions on Social Media." https://searchenginejournal.com/tools-track-brand-mentions-social-media/303287/#close (accessed December 2019).

Hahn, I. undated. "10 B2B Social Media Strategies that Work for Any Industry." https://blog.hubspot.com/blog/tabid/6307/bid/32765/how-b2b-marketers-can-succeed-on-the-6-big-social-networks.aspx (accessed December 2019).

Chapter 3

Carey, I. October 9, 2019. "Why is WiFi at Events so Bad?" https://skift.com/2019/10/09/why-is-wi-fi-at-events-still-so-bad/, (accessed December 2019).

Greenwald, W. May 15, 2019. "What Is 8K? Should You Buy a New TV or Wait?" https://pcmag.com/article/358604/what-is-8k-should-you-buy-a-new-tv-or-wait, (accessed December 2019).

Ball, Corbin, Expert, Writer and Lecturer on Event Technology. January 17, 2020. "E-mail Message to Author."

Sarcinella, P. 2019. "Senior Director of Sales at Millenium Technology Group, Phone Interview with Author." November 22, 2019.

Livengood, C. February 20, 2019. "Chemical Bank buys naming rights to Cobo Center." https://crainsdetroit.com/banking/chemical-bank-buys-naming-rights-cobo-center (accessed September 2019).

Chapter 4

Investopedia. Undated. "Overhead" https://investopedia.com/terms/o/overhead. asp (accessed December 2019).

Chapter 6

International Association of Venue Managers. 2016. "Exhibitions and Meetings Safety and Security Initiative – Convention Center Security Guide (Draft)."

King, S.V. July 8, 2018. "11 Warning Signs of Workers Compensation Insurance Fraud." cpapracticeadvisor.com/small-business/news/12419587/11-warning-signs-of-workers-compensation-insurance-fraud (accessed September 2019).

Chapter 8

CallCentreHelper.Com. April 27, 2016. Modified September 19, 2019. "How Do I… Measure Employee Engagement?" https://callcentrehelper.com/how-do-i-measure-employee-engagement-84173.htm (accessed October 2019).

Custominsight. Undated. "What is Employee Satisfaction?" https://custominsight.com/employee-engagement-survey/what-is-employee-satisfaction.asp (accessed October 2019).

Harper, J. August 26, 2018. "Employee Engagement on the Rise in the U.S." https://news.gallup.com/poll/241649/employee-engagement-rise.aspx (accessed October 2019).

Chapter 10

School of Arts, University of Leicester. Undated. "Presenting Numerical Data." https://www2.le.ac.uk/offices/ld/resources/numericaldata/numericaldata, (accessed October 2019).

Tufted, E.R. 1983. *The Visual Display of Quantitative Information*. Cheshire CT, Graphics Press, LLC.

Barcelona Field Study Centre. Undated. "Data Presentation: Bar Charts." https://geographyfieldwork.com/DataPresentationBarCharts.htm (accessed September 2019).

Better Evaluation. undated. "Line Charts" https://betterevaluation.org/en/evaluation-options/LineGraph (accessed September 2019).

Paudyal, N. July 7, 2016. "8 Reasons Why Typography Is Important." https://engadget.com/2016/07/17/8-reasons-why-typography-is-important/ (accessed September 2019).

Friend, J. undated. "Why Did Microsoft Change The Default Font To Calibri?" https://forbes.com/sites/quora/2013/12/18/why-did-microsoft-change-the-default-font-to-calibri/#2f2a78a93e06 (accessed September 2019).

Kosara, R. March 17, 2013. "A Better Definition of Chart Junk." https://eagereyes.org/blog/2013/definition-chart-junk (accessed September 2019).

Spacey, J. February 13, 2017. "8 Examples of Chart Junk." https://simplicable.com/new/chartjunk (accessed September 2019).

Alexander, M. 2016. Excel Dashboards and Reports for Dummies, Chichester West Sussex UK, John Wiley & Sons.

Logianalytics. undated. "Dashboard Design Fundamentals." https://logianalytics.com/dashboarddesignguide/dashboard-design-fundamentals/ (accessed September 2019).

Shaw, G., R. Brown, and P. Bromley. May–June 1998. "Strategic Stories: How 3M Is Rewriting Business Planning." https://hbr.org/1998/05/strategic-stories-how-3m-is-rewriting-business-planning (accessed September 2019).

Chapter 11

EDUCBA. Undated. "Power BI vs. Excel." https://educba.com/power-bi-vs-excel/ (accessed October 2019).

Clifton, J., and J. Harter. 2019. It's the Manager, New York, Gallup Press.

Chapter 12

Kohl, O. September 19, 2019. "An End to KPI Misdirection: Aligning Data to Strategy+." https://rtinsights.com/the-case-for-orchestrated-kpis/ (accessed December 2019).

Calanca, T. 2019. "Executive Vice President for Exhibitions, Informar, Phone Interview with Author." (accessed November 12 2019).

Shaw, G.B. undated. https://allauthor.com/quotes/31215/ (accessed December 2019).

The COVID - 19 Pandemic

Hazinski, T. April 17, 2020."HVS COVID - 19 Impact on Lodging Tax Revenues".https://hotel-online.com/press_releases/release/hvs-covid-19-impact-on-lodging-tax-revenues/. (accessed May, 2020).

Radnofsky, L. and Cohen, B. "Sports Eye Second Wave as New Risk". The Wall Street Journal, April 18-19, 2020.

Garcia, J. July 2, 2020. "Visit Orlando handed out nearly $300,000 in extra pay as hotel taxes plummeted because of coronavirus". https://www.orlandosentinel.com/news/os-ne-visit-orlando-bonuses-20200702-nncwfqybsveezgnlihzpp7orti-story.html. (accessed July, 2020).

Camus, A. 1947. www.goodreads.com/quotes/147920

About the Author

Myles McGrane's business career started at the National Broadcasting Company in New York where he held energy and facility management positions. After NBC he joined Ogden Corporation's Entertainment Division where he was instrumental in organizing the private management of the Javits Center and was moved frequently to assist with troubled accounts. Following Ogden Corporation, he joined a new management team at the Javits Center as General Manager. The team was charged with reforming a notorious union labor situation and rebuilding the Center's declining business. He was a key player in re-negotiating all the labor contracts, and hiring and training a new workforce (up to 2,000 employees) without business disruption. During his 12-year tenure as General Manager, the Javits Center operated profitably each year and built a sizable capital reserve. His achievements were recognized and he was named one of the "Top 100 Most Influential" people in the trade show industry by *Trade Show Week* magazine in 2004 and 2006. He then left the Javits Center and joined Centerplate as Corporate Vice President of Facility Design and Management. Centerplate is a top-tier concession and catering company serving only the sports and entertainment sector.

In July 2009 he formed MTMConsult, LLC, a consultancy offering strategic business advice to the convention and trade show and facility management sectors. Clients have included St. Johns University, Washington DC Convention Center, The America's Center (St. Louis), Advanstar Communications, UBM, Cobo Hall (Detroit), Centerplate, Merchandise Mart Properties and others. His assignments have ranged from project management of a university's campus high-voltage infrastructure, to advising on union labor issues, to strategic planning and new business development.

He was educated at the U.S. Naval Academy in Annapolis where he received BS in Naval Science. His military service followed as a Navy pilot. He also earned an MS degree in City Planning from the University of Tennessee.

Index

OTHER TITLES IN THE TOURISM AND HOSPITALITY MANAGEMENT COLLECTION

Betsy Bender Stringam, New Mexico State University, Editor

- *Cultural and Heritage Tourism and Management* by Tammie J. Kaufman
- *Marine Tourism, Climate Change, and Resilience in the Caribbean, Volume II* by Kreg Ettenger and Samantha Hogenson
- *Marketing Essentials for Independent Lodging* by Pamela Lanier and Marie Lanier
- *Marine Tourism, Climate Change, and Resiliency in the Caribbean, Volume I* by Kreg Ettenger and Samantha Hogenson
- *Catering and Convention Service Survival Guide in Hotels and Casinos* by Lisa Lynn Backus and Patti J. Shock
- *Coastal Tourism, Sustainability, and Climate Change in the Caribbean, Volume II* by Martha Honey and Kreg Ettenger
- *Coastal Tourism, Sustainability, and Climate Change in the Caribbean, Volume I* by Martha Honey and Kreg Ettenger
- *The Good Company* by Robert Girling and Heather Gordy

Concise and Applied Business Books

The Collection listed above is one of 30 business subject collections that Business Expert Press has grown to make BEP a premiere publisher of print and digital books. Our concise and applied books are for...

- Professionals and Practitioners
- Faculty who adopt our books for courses
- Librarians who know that BEP's Digital Libraries are a unique way to offer students ebooks to download, not restricted with any digital rights management
- Executive Training Course Leaders
- Business Seminar Organizers

Business Expert Press books are for anyone who needs to dig deeper on business ideas, goals, and solutions to everyday problems. Whether one print book, one ebook, or buying a digital library of 110 ebooks, we remain the affordable and smart way to be business smart. For more information, please visit www.businessexpertpress.com, or contact sales@businessexpertpress.com.